Advance Praise for Remember Who You Are

"This book offers a poetic and profound affirmation of the divine with us—a vital companion as we travel the great journey of consciously evolving."
—Jacquelyn Small, author and founding director of the Eupsychia Institute

"*Remember Who You Are* is an exquisitely beautiful book. It ignites poignant memories and stimulates individual insights for everyone's own journey. It is timeless, archetypal, poetic, and meaningful."
—Angeles Arrien, Ph.D., cultural anthropologist and author of *The Second Half of Life*

"Absolutely exquisite! *Remember Who You Are* is a beautiful, practical, and inspiring guide for the journey of self-discovery. This is a book that speaks to the difficulties and complexities as well as to the delights and the ultimate simplicity of the voyage. It is truly a book to treasure."
—Hal Stone, Ph.D. & Sidra Stone, Ph.D., authors of *Partnering: A New Kind of Relationship*

"*Remember Who You Are* is an exquisitely comforting book, compiled and narrated by the gifted and generous Linda Carroll. Each page holds sensitive nuggets of necessary wisdom; each chapter unfolds with clarity and helpful guidance. If you know anyone who needs to be befriended by her own story right now—who could use a little help accepting whatever difficult or unexpected things have come her way, as well as the blessings we often forget to notice enough—or if that person is yourself—this is the book to hold close."
—Naomi Shihab Nye, author of *19 Varieties of Gazelle* and *Words Under the Words*

"*Remember Who You Are* helps the reader do just that—at the deepest level. An artfully woven tapestry of personal reflection, questions for the reader, and words of the world's great sages, this book is an intimate guide for anyone seeking greater spiritual depth. The book not only offers pages of inspiration; it also is a practical guide for forming a women's circle. In whatever form, it integrates some of the most thoughtful spiritual and psychological teachings of our day."
—Helen LaKelly Hunt, Ph.D., coauthor of *Receiving Love*

Remember Who You Are

Seven Stages on a Woman's Journey of Spirit

———⚬———

LINDA CARROLL

Conari Press

First published in 2008 by Conari Press,
an imprint of Red Wheel/Weiser, LLC
With offices at:
500 Third Street, Suite 230
San Francisco, CA 94107
www.redwheelweiser.com

ISBN: 978-1-57324-367-4
Library of Congress Cataloging-in-Publication Data
Carroll, Linda.
Remember who you are : seven stages on a woman's journey of spirit / Linda
Carroll.
p. cm.
ISBN 978-1-57324-367-4 (alk. paper)
1. Women--Religious life. I. Title.
BL625.7.C365 2008
204'.4082—dc22
2008029761

Cover and text design by Jessica Dacher
Typeset in Nevia BT Pro and Goudy
Author photograph © Karen Ruckman

TCP
10 9 8 7 6 5 4 3 2 1

My song is of the generations, it echoes
the old dialogue of the years; it is the tribal
chorus that no one may sing alone.
— LAURIS EDMONDS

This book is dedicated to
the women in my family:

My mother, Paula Fox

My daughters, Jaimee King,
Nicole Carroll, and Courtney Love

My granddaughters, Maria Fox Menely,
Katherine Nicole King, and Frances Cobain

My daughter-in-law, Margaret Ronda

Louelle Risi and Honey Hanna, who first showed
me the delight of friendship between women

And Sylva, who is never far away.

Contents

INTRODUCTION   11

PART I   The Spiritual Connection

   Chapter 1   The Golden Cord   17

   Chapter 2   The Human Search   22

PART II   The Path

   Chapter 3   Forgetting   33

   Chapter 4   Remembering   43

   Chapter 5   Exploring   55

   Chapter 6   Practicing   66

   Chapter 7   Shadows on the Path   74

   Chapter 8   Reclaiming   84

   Chapter 9   Acceptance   93

   Chapter 10 Using *Remember Who You Are*   98
               in a Women's Group

The Journey

One day you finally knew
what you had to do, and began,
though the voices around you
kept shouting
their bad advice—
though the whole house
began to tremble
and you felt the old tug
at your ankles.
"Mend my life!"
each voice cried.
But you didn't stop.
You knew what you had to do,
though the wind pried
with its stiff fingers
at the very foundations—
though their melancholy
was terrible.
It was already late
enough, and a wild night,
and the road full of fallen
branches and stones.
But little by little,
as you left their voices behind,
the stars began to burn
through the sheets of clouds,
and there was a new voice,
which you slowly
recognized as your own,
that kept you company
as you strode deeper and deeper
into the world,
determined to do
the only thing you could do—
determined to save
the only life you could save.

— MARY OLIVER, "THE JOURNEY"

Introduction

———∞———

To live is so startling,
It leaves little time for
Anything else.
— EMILY DICKINSON

This book presents a framework, in seven stages, to describe and affirm women's spiritual journeys. Looking at the phases of women's lives across time and cultures, in poems, plays, photographs, or personal stories, we see a shared spiritual essence. Yet we often forget our connection with this essence in our everyday lives. Remembering who we truly are is our life's work. This book is a reflection of the author's personal discoveries and other women's stories about the journey of recollection, reconnection, and recovery. Throughout the book, the universal longing for and connection to the essential spirit is celebrated, not only with prose, but through poetry.

The book is light, a feather, a promise. It hopes to reveal footprint *and* path, to offer a practical guide to exploring the spiritual dimension, including its difficulties and pitfalls. The book navigates seven stages on this journey. Often the stages overlap, circle back, and intertwine, forming a pattern that reflects the multifaceted quality of the feminine spirit.

The Seven Stages

Forgetting, or losing the connection to essential spiritual self, happens when we are born and enter the physical world. We develop a personality that allows us to adapt to our family and society. This original self is rarely remembered, although at times we catch glimpses of it. Moments of unexpected grace—falling in love, acting from certainty rather than fear—are reminders. We reconnect with our essence, too, when our senses are moved by the natural world around us.

Remembering is the key to most world religions and to spiritual experience. It may be prompted by a thought, a poem, a luminous dream, a dramatic event such as a mystical experience, or any transition or change. In whatever way we are awakened, we are reminded for a moment of a different realm of existence with its own truth. Such revelations often signify the beginning of the journey back to essence.

Exploring spiritual ideas and religious practices moves us toward an awareness of remembering. We participate in traditional and unfamiliar forms of prayer, join women's circles within churches, temples, and community organizations, or attend retreats and seminars. Most bookstores now have an entire section devoted to "women's spirituality," reflecting an ever-widening acceptance of a new phase in women's history. Even the practice of pilgrimage (visiting sacred sites throughout the world) is undergoing a revival in our culture.

Practicing allows us to begin using rituals that can put us on the spiritual path each day. Some traditions use ceremonies, liturgies, prayers, or meditation at a specific time and place; some embrace a lifestyle that itself becomes the practice. Without practice, the treasures we have found will almost surely lose their light and promise. With practice, the spiritual can entwine with the everyday, changing our sense of ourselves and the world in fundamental ways.

Shadows on the Path reflects on obstacles that will confront us, for this path meanders through as many low roads as high, and dips deeply into the world of emotions and innermost thoughts, even those we previously thought unacceptable. We may feel grief for all the time we have lost in failing to attend to our deeper needs. Difficulties may emerge, too, in our relationships with others as we try to communicate what we discover. Our friends and loved ones may not understand—may even be threatened by—who we are becoming as we recognize our truer nature.

Reclaiming is that stage in which we begin to recognize and trust those things that have meaning for us, and we take hold of the direction of our lives, both inside and out. Being honest with ourselves and others is more consequential now. We are more accountable for our actions. Sometimes we are even able to challenge others and ourselves with more ease and less judgment, feeling greater compassion for our common difficulties. At the end of most stories about a sacred journey, the voyager returns with hard-earned wisdom and many gifts for her community. We may find ourselves in the same work and relationships, but standing on new ground, seeing life through new lenses.

Accepting is less a stage than a condition woven throughout the stages. It is the knowledge that we never completely "arrive." We are always on the path. We are always forgetting, remembering, exploring, practicing, integrating, and then forgetting again. Acknowledging this, we learn to accept the inevitability of lapsing into old responses with limited ways of seeing. We develop more patience and empathy, more humor about our human fragility, and greater tolerance for having to find our way back again and again.

There is a Native American folktale that claims each person is born into this world with a special song that is his or hers alone. It is my hope that this book will remind readers that we each have a song, and will inspire us all to bring forth its music.

— LINDA CARROLL

PART I

The Spiritual
Connection

Chapter 1

The Golden Cord

———— ✖ ————

A woman stands by a window on a sweet spring morning and she weeps for something she cannot name. She has everything she imagined she could ever want, yet on this day she is empty and filled with a yearning that has no face. Feeling in the world but not of it, she performs the tasks of everyday life in a solitude that enfolds her like a cocoon.

The woman in the window is not alone. No matter what culture or spiritual tradition we are born into, human beings share her yearning. Our universal legacy of poetry, myth, and story suggests that we are born connected to something beyond what we consciously recognize as reality—often called Spirit, God, Higher Power, Intuition, Essence. It is this mysterious connection that William Wordsworth writes of in his "Ode to Immortality":

Our birth is but a sleep and a forgetting:
The Soul that rises with us, our life's Star,
Hath had elsewhere its setting,

And cometh from afar:
Not in entire forgetfulness,
And not in utter nakedness,
But trailing clouds of glory do we come
From God, who is our home . . .

As we become part of the human community, we lose a sense of our spiritual connection. Across cultures, in stories and myth, heroes and heroines search for this missing sense of "home." Wordsworth describes this forgetting in this way:

There was a time when meadow, grove, and stream,
The earth, and every common sight,
To me did seem
Appareled in celestial light,
The glory and the freshness of a dream.
It is not now as it hath been of yore;—
Turn wheresoe'er I may,
By night or day,
The things which I have seen I now can see no more.

What is this "celestial light" we once knew? Why do we stop seeing it? How can we find it again?

We search for answers outside ourselves for a long time before we realize we are looking in the wrong direction. Legends portray the seeker climbing the tallest mountains and searching the deepest oceans for silver and gold. After a long and difficult passage, the heroine realizes the real treasure is something she had all along. The Holy Grail goes by many names, but it is her own spirit she seeks.

What is the human spirit? Spirit, the vital principle or animating force within living beings, is one of many words that attempt to grasp the enormity of what a person is beyond the narrative that defines him or her in a particular place and time. We refer to Spirit as a spark, perhaps because it reflects a glimmer of recognition that rises when we hear the word. Maybe it is a bit of brilliance from the place we come from.

Can we listen to the breeze without calling it breeze?
Talking together we have to use words
so that we can listen together, but the listening is not the words. the
listening is openness to what's not knowable.
— TONI PACKER, MEDITATION TEACHER

Although definition eludes us, when Spirit fills us, we feel buoyant, complete, and alive. We have direction. Life is meaningful. And when we are empty of Spirit, we feel bereft, depressed, oppressed, and, like the woman in the window, lonely and longing. The deepest wish of the human heart is to know that Spirit, that essential, original self. If we can remember who we really are, the connection will sustain us through times of greatest challenge.

A Native American legend says we are born with an invisible golden cord that connects the top of our heads to the Spirit world from which we came. This cord of gold helps us in our passage to the human world. As infants, when we are frightened, tired, or bewildered, we draw strength from it. As the skin thickens, covering the fontanel on our infant skulls in the first months of life, the cord gets smaller. Finally it disappears. We forget all we have known of our own true self as we enter fully into the world of families, community, and culture. Remembering that essence, reestablishing connection to that "invisible golden cord," is what I believe to be the purpose of each human life.

Experiencing our lives in a physical body, we are engulfed and encased by early events and circumstances. When we smile at Mother, she smiles back. That feels good, so we do it again. When we run into the street, Father gets upset. This is frightening, and we don't repeat our mistake. Then influences beyond our immediate families develop the socialized person we are becoming. We learn more about life, love, and personal values from peers, school, movies, songs, and by watching the relationships around us. We create beliefs about who we are based on what we understand the world to be and what others tell us we are.

As we grow accustomed to the outside world of rules, beliefs, and structures, we forget that our Spirit has its own truth, set of laws, and wisdom, our essence. We often think all we are is a social construct. Though we may refer to our "origins," we stop short of the source of truth that resides deep and forgotten inside us. Yet this inner presence is the well from which our highest humanity and deepest wisdom is drawn. A woman's rediscovery of her essence begins with a journey to remember and reclaim this source.

Home is a metaphor for our inner life. The woman in the window who has lost her way is every woman who longs for connection within. Paradoxically, a sacred relationship to our home—to ourselves and our inner lives—can begin with departure. We must leave home to come home. In leaving, we lose nothing, but in finding the home that was lost, we gain everything.

> You may say "existence," but you can't grasp it!
> You may say "nonexistence," but many things appear!
> It is beyond the sky of "existence" and "nonexistence"
> — DAKINI LION-FACE

Reflection Questions

> And I write it to you
> at this moment
> never being able to get
> the essence
>   the true breath
>
> in words, because we exist
> not in words, but in motion
> set off by them, by

the simple flight of crow
and by us
in our loving
— JOY HARJO, "MOTION"

↝ How do you define Spirit?

↝ How do you define Soul?

↝ How do you define Essence?

↝ What does it mean to you to "Remember Who You Are"? What qualities do you consider to be a part of your essential self?

Look at pictures of yourself as a child that reflect your essential qualities. Describe what you see in the child's activities, body, or eyes that recalls these essential, magical qualities.

Familiar childhood stories teach that we must leave home to find home; the happy ending requires we discover the mystery within. Sleeping Beauty wakes up, Pinocchio becomes a real boy, and Dorothy returns to Kansas, discovering that what she sought was in the place she left. Can you think of a journey you took, where you had to leave your outer life to discover a part of your inner self?

Chapter 2

The Human Search

——⧓——

Why—do they shut Me out of Heaven?
Did I sing—too loud?
– EMILY DICKINSON

Humans enter this life without answers to the most important questions about the nature of their existence:

Who am I?
What am I doing here?
Is there a God?
Did I exist before my first breath?
Do I exist after my last?

These questions are all in the realm of the Spirit. For many people spirituality means religion; for others it refers to an invisible force beyond the conscious mind, a physical or mental state in which one feels an unseen source of energy and support. The spiritual dimension is not usually articulated through ordinary language or understood through reason alone. In *The Little Prince*, Antoine de Saint-Exupery suggests an approach to this dimension: "And now here is my secret, a very simple secret: It is only with the heart that one can see rightly; what is essential is invisible to the eye."

We know the spiritual world largely through means other than language, the brain's domain. In the language of Spirit, we "see through the heart." We use metaphors, dreams, symbols, fables, and stories to define it. We use art and poetry. A sunset. Pounding surf. All of these remind us we are a part of something greater than ourselves.

Stories and Myths

As we search for meaning, we tell stories about who we are and what we believe. These stories help define our current lives, our past and future, and the meaning we make of life itself.

The history of our families is made up of stories, some that pre-date our birth, some about relationships among family members, and some in which we are in our strengths and weaknesses the stars of the tales. We tell and retell stories about events that were wounding, satisfying, thrilling, or frightening. Over time, family lore becomes absolute, like photographs, and these snapshots are transformed into a sort of internal home movie, seamless from beginning to end, re-played over and over.

We tell other stories. We have narratives that demonstrate our deepest fears, express our greatest dreams, and are the source of our personal ideals.

Our outlook is like a lens. Our vision of the world depends on the color of the lens we are looking through. Here is an example. When Elizabeth was eighteen months old, she wandered away from a family picnic and fell into a creek. A friend's German shepherd found her there and barked until someone came. She was raised with the story of how the dog saved her life. At about the same age, her friend Julia was bitten by a similar kind of dog. Much later in life, the two friends met in front of a café. A German shepherd came walking up to them. Elizabeth smiled and reached out to stroke it. Julia stepped back, pale and visibly shaken. Both responses had more to do with the lens through which they saw the dog than with the dog itself.

Of course, our "lens" does not tell us *the* "truth." But because it is the prism through which we are looking, it appears to be true to us, and we filter new information and feelings through it.

If they see
breasts and long hair coming
(they) call it woman,

if beard and whiskers
they call it man:

but, look, the self that hovers
in between
is neither man
nor woman

O Rāmanātha
— A. K. RAMANUJAN, "DEVARA DASIMAYYATR"

On a far larger scale, myths are stories that grow out of the human search for meaning. They help us to understand passages and trials from birth until death and are clues to the possibilities of the human spirit.

Joseph Campbell, the American mythologist and scholar, was fascinated by the different images and ideas of Divinity he found throughout his career. These worldwide images embodied many of the same themes. Campbell called them "the masks of God," which carry clues to the spiritual aspects common to all humans.

Though the mystery of life may be beyond our understanding, these archetypal stories carry the message that there is an invisible place, a spiritual plane, from which we are separated by only a very thin veil known as the conscious mind. Religions and spiritual leaders say that we must make an effort to look behind the veil to fulfill our life's purpose. Holy Scriptures and countless tales and legends describe this transformation of consciousness. You have looked at things in one way, and now you will see them differently. Reconnecting with those stories becomes one way of seeing our lives anew, and of finding the answers that we all seek.

The Breath inside the Breath

Although we are born into this world without a roadmap to plot our way, we are given clues, one of which is breath and breathing. The Greek word "pneuma" means both spirit and breath. Like a curtain, our first breath hides everything that happened to us before birth, and whatever may follow our final breath. Breath is at once essential and mysterious. Perhaps this is why many forms of spirituality look to breath awareness as a source of wisdom. We may watch the effortless way in which "the breath breathes us," observing it as though we are a "witness" to it. We may consciously "breathe the breath," slowing down or speeding up, as practiced in various forms of yoga, martial arts, meditation, and biofeedback. Our breath provides an index of how comfortable we are in the moment. When we are afraid, we tighten our bodies and breathe faster; when relaxed, we soften and breathe slowly.

> *Student, tell me, what is God?*
> *He is the breath inside the breath.*
> — KABIR

Regardless of culture, environment, and personal history, humans share the legacy of birth, death, and the common yearning to make meaning of the time in between. Wouldn't it be clever to hide the secret of life in this first and final human experience of breath?

Flower, Fruit, and Seed

For women, another answer to life's meaning might be found in the mysteries of our unique life cycles. Celtic tradition, for example, recognizes three cycles in a woman's lifetime: the flower (the girl), the fruit (the mother), and the seed (the elder). In many cultures, each transition is considered a sacred event that is honored with rituals.

The Flower

From a very young age, women absorb familial and cultural attitudes about our bodies. As we enter adolescence and our bodies change, we become more consciously attuned to the sexual side of our nature. We begin to menstruate and hormones surge through us, directing our attention ever more overtly to the wonders and torment of sexual attraction.

> *The texture of twilight made me think of*
> *Lengths of Dotted Swiss. In my room*
> *I wrapped scarred knees in dresses*
> *That once went to big-band dances;*
> *I baptized my earlobes with rosewater.*
> *Along the window-sill, the lipstick stubs*
> *Glittered in their steel shells.*
> — RITA DOVE, "ADOLESCENCE—III"

The Fruit

The fruit of a woman's life is her fertility. The ability to give birth connects us directly to the greatest mystery and wonder, the source of life itself. Most females share this connection, whether we have children or not. We bring new life into the world through our physical and creative bodies and nurture and grow it. In our tradition, women's biology has often been pathologized. Premenstrual syndrome is an endless source of tasteless jokes, and women are taught to be embarrassed about their monthly "curse." In some cultures, however, the seasons of a woman's reproductive life are intimately bound to her relationship with the sacred. In some Native American traditions, women take time away from ordinary life during their monthly cycles in a ritual of wisdom seeking.

The Seed

When you age, you become wiser in so many ways. You make adjustments for having less stamina, but you know in your mind what you can achieve. Experience has shown you the potential of the human spirit. Committing to what is right, what is just, and what is good.
— CORETTA SCOTT KING

This time in a woman's life is signified by menopause. Reproductive forces no longer control us. Now there is time to look inward.

The sense of spirituality that seems to increase with age is not necessarily religious. As I watch my eight grandchildren grow and actually be there, existing and full of life, I realize that the Holocaust didn't work.
— ELAINE ALEXANDER

We may joke about hot flashes and memory loss, but this season offers possibilities for reclaiming ourselves. As menopause ceases, the body discovers a new vigor.

Though I am weak and tired now,
And my youthful step long gone,
Leaning on this staff,
I climb the mountain peak. My cloak cast off, my bowl overturned,
I sit here on this rock.
And over my spirit blows
The breath
  Of liberty I've won the triple gems.
The Buddha's way is mine.
— METTIKA, BUDDHIST NUN, SIXTH CENTURY BC

Circle of the Spirit

The Judeo-Christian tradition teaches to look up and out for God, climbing Jacob's ladder from the Book of Genesis. Joan Borysenko, an author and psychologist, has introduced a feminine variation on that tradition she calls Sarah's circle. On the ladder, the path to God is linear, logical; Sarah's circle is relational and intuitive. Like Earth-based traditions and Goddess cultures, the circle instead offers women a way to honor innate gifts.

As ancient as the wind and as timeless as the ocean is the story of the female rediscovering her Essence. This is our story too, as we travel on our passage home.

Reflection Questions

I was looking at the flower bed by the front door; "That is the whole," I said. I was looking at a plant with a spread of leaves; and it seemed suddenly plain that the flower itself was a part of the earth; that a ring enclosed what was the flower; and that was the real flower; part earth; part flower.
— VIRGINIA WOOLF

⤳ What do you think it means to "see with the heart"? Where in your current life can you do this the easiest? Where is it the most difficult?

⤳ Sally's mother used to say "Suffer, suffer straight ahead." What was your mother's favorite saying about life? What was your father's?

⤳ What do you imagine people would say is your most commonly used expression?

⤳ Can you think of a way you once viewed a relationship, work, or dreams in your life that seemed to be the "absolute truth"? Remember the process by which they changed and you saw the same person, relationship, or dream through "a different lens"? Which was the true lens?

⤳ How do you experience your desire to nurture life? Through some creative expression with writing, art, or dance? By supporting your family or friends? In relationship to pets, gardening, building or at work? List how you express your nurturing aspects.

⤳ What are you looking for as you begin this journey? What calls you to embark on this journey now?

PART II

The Path

If female history is different, if female biology is different, if female psychology is different, if all the hundreds of little responses to life's daily occurrences are different, how can the spirituality be the same?
— THERESA KING

Chapter 3

Forgetting

———— ✧ ————

I turned my face for a moment, and it became my life.
— ANONYMOUS WOMAN

Imagine yourself inside your mother's womb. You are floating in an ocean of bliss. Food and oxygen are effortlessly consumed in just the right amounts—you don't even have to breathe for yourself. After nine months, this perfect world changes without warning. Your warm water home disappears, the birth canal narrows, and the sanctuary that was once a shelter is now a cave of danger and suffering. There is only one way out, as your mother labors to bring you into the world. When her cervix expands and the journey of birth begins, you feel an intolerable pressure on the top of your skull. The walls of the cavern are caving in; contractions are pushing you out into the unknown. Then your body experiences air and light for the first time, the umbilical cord is cut, separating you from your mother, and you take your first breath. In the best of circumstances, you are handed back to your mother and experience relief.

You are introduced to new pleasure, as you feel your parents' welcome through touch and sound, smell your mother's familiar scent, and taste her sweet milk. You also are introduced to pain. Your eyes have unfamiliar chemicals squirted into them; a needle stings your tiny foot as it draws blood, and if you are separated from your mother, or put in an incubator alone, you may feel bewilderment and fear. Your senses are overwhelmed, your body is weary, and your recollection of where you have come from fades.

Each of us experiences birth differently, but it is always an ordeal, banished from utopia to a strange new land. Once it is over, we have survived our first trauma, variations of which will occur throughout life until the final crossing back through the mystery of death. Adapting to this new life takes our attention away from what is happening inside, from our deepest emotions, perceptions, and connection to the spirit we came from.

Gradually, ordinary experience in the outside world overlays our relationship to the one within. Yet this other self remains unchanged, defining our individuality like a spiritual fingerprint. Perhaps this is why a new baby, a soft black puppy, or a breaking yellow bud on a forsythia branch takes our breath away. Without realizing it, we are responding to Spirit. Such images that we draw from our everyday surroundings can remind us of our deepest being, which we cannot always access directly. We may also recover these initial memories through metaphors, dreams, and images of nature.

> Once in the dream of a night I stood
> Lone in the light of a magical wood,
> Soul-deep in visions that poppy-like sprang;
> And spirits of Truth were the birds that sang
> — SAROJINI NAIDU

From our very first breath, we live in two worlds: the outer, material one governed by laws of space, time, and culture, and the inner one of imagery, intuition, and spirit. The inner world retreats but does not disappear. We glimpse it in fairy tales, myths, and legends. We visit it through our dreams and in the realm of imagination.

Religion helps us remember the best of our inner world, but it can also close us off from our spiritual core.

> *They dunked me in the creek;*
> *a tiny brooklet.*
> *Muddy, gooey with rotting leaves,*
> *a greenish mold floating;*
> *definable.*
> *For love it was. For love of God*
> *at seven. All in white.*
> *With God's mud ruining my snowy*
> *socks and his bullfrog spoors*
> *gluing up my face.*
> — ALICE WALKER, "BAPTISM"

As infants, we depend entirely upon others. To get our needs met as quickly and safely as possible, we must pay attention to cues in the outer world. One infant finds results in yelling and demanding. Another discovers that smiling and cooing bring the fastest response. In our drive for survival, security, safety, bonding, and approval, we look to others for clues on how to best behave.

Families and cultures impress on us what to believe in and what to value. If you were born on a cattle ranch in Montana, you would see cattle as a source of food, and breeding them as an honorable way to make a living. If you were raised in a Hindu family in India, you would see the same cattle as representatives of the holiest of deities, never to be consumed. Thus, we are all born with a unique spirit and the similar essential qualities, but much of this inner Self becomes marked by the factors of our family life and culture.

Our upbringing also has a tremendous impact on how we evaluate our own intuition, creativity, and intelligence. In the small Missouri town she grew up in, Jennifer's best friend was her cousin, Beth. They were born just four months apart, looked similar, and as little girls secretly believed they were identical twins. In the fourth grade, to her deep distress, Jennifer was told she would not be continuing on to the fifth grade with the rest of her classmates. She had done well in school and didn't understand why she was being held back. Her teacher and parents assured her, however, that the decision was in her best interests, and she remembers them saying, "We just don't think you are keeping up."

In the ensuing years, the choices Jennifer made about what schools to attend, what jobs to take, and what kind of partner she was worthy of were all rooted in that early experience. Eventually, she entered therapy because she was tired of uninspiring jobs and relationships in which she didn't feel valued. Impressed by her intelligence, her therapist was puzzled that she had been held back in school and asked Jennifer to inquire with her family about that decision made years ago. Shortly thereafter, she came to her appointment visibly shaken. She had discovered that her parents and teachers had been concerned that the closeness between her and Beth might be unhealthy and that the two should be separated. Because no other school existed in their little town, and Jennifer was the younger of the two cousins, they decided to hold her back a year. They told her she was backward only to justify what they did. Unfortunately, she believed them and then spent the next thirty years assuming that she wasn't quick or smart enough to create the life she really wanted. She had built her life around a feeling of inadequacy.

Our personalities are formed by many such beliefs. The word personality stems from the Greek word "persona," which means mask. The origin is apt, because our personalities are similar to masks. They show one side to the outside world, even as another side lies just beneath. As we grow up, we develop variations of these faces to show to different people.

Over time our attitudes, beliefs, and behaviors become molded to the contours of each mask we wear. Psychologists Hal and Sidra Stone have spent their lives studying and teaching about these masks, which they call "the psychology of selves." We have many of these unique "selves" within us, each with its own history, beliefs, and behavior. Our "pleaser" shows herself to be helpful, as she thinks this is the best way to be liked. A "protector" makes choices that offer the greatest safety. A "critic" tells us what's wrong before someone else does.

We are taught that certain parts of ourselves are not acceptable and need to be hidden. These commonly disowned aspects may be our envy, aggression, our erotic and sensual impulses, or what we judge in ourselves to be pitiful. We want to be seen by others as successful, happy, funny, on top of everything. Thus, we often refuse to acknowledge deeper truths about ourselves, fearing they may be too painful or ugly to address.

To make matters worse, our culture often teaches us that "finding ourselves" is also a matter of finding "the right partner." We are encouraged to dwell in romantic fantasies by endless messages from songs and movies that reinforce this. We are instructed to look outward for happiness, and thus we often look to someone else to be the "right person" instead of turning inward where the real "right person" is waiting to be discovered.

> *I dreamed how it would happen:*
> *He would meet me by the blue spruce,*
> *A carnation over his heart, saying,*
> *"I have come for you, madam;*
> *I have loved you in my dreams."*
> — RITA DOVE, "ADOLESCENCE—III"

As children, girls often receive a variety of gender-specific messages, which further separate them from their true selves. Affiliation, relatedness, and cooperation are frequently rewarded. And then there is the part about being beautiful, which we are taught equals worthiness. Aggression and competition may be discouraged, and no matter how hard many women may fight to change the patriarchal beliefs about the superior authority of men, many of the attitudes are so internalized that we are not even aware we hold them.

Sensation and feelings distract us from our original self: pain, pleasure, anger, sorrow, fear, and happiness. We manage our feelings with a variety of personas, many of which we believe protect us from life's hurts, and we begin to consider these masks to be who we truly are.

> You must try,
> the voice said, to become colder.
> I understood at once.
> It is like the bodies of gods; cast in bronze,
> braced in stone. Only something heartless
> could bear the full weight.
> — JANE HIRSHFIELD, "THE WORLD LOVED BY MOONLIGHT"

It is important to stress that creating protections and defenses is not bad or wrong. Our masks protect us from real and imagined harm and are often necessary to survive in the world. But problems arise when we believe we are nothing more than our masks.

We experience our lost connection to our true nature as a hole in need of filling. We search for the right job, the "One" person, a big bank account, or a perfect body. When that doesn't work, we may go for other kinds of fillers, such as alcohol, drugs, sex, and constant drama. Along the way, if we dare to look deep enough beneath the masks, we may be reminded that another life awaits us.

> No more masks! No more mythologies!
> Now for the first time, the god lifts his hand,
> The fragments join in me with their own music.
> — MURIEL RUKEYSER, "THE POEM AS MASK, ORPHEUS"

Imagine a large forest filled with trees, flowers, rivers, unlimited creatures, and plants. You are allowed to explore only one-tenth of the kingdom. What lies outside the permitted sliver of land, the forest caretakers tell you, is dangerous, forbidden, or perhaps does not even exist. And so you live your life within the bounds of the allotted area. At times you yearn—and at other times fear—to know what lies beyond. But more often than not, you simply forget anything might lie out there at all.

Each of us is such a forest. We live in a very small part of who we are. Yet something in us longs for more. We celebrate stories about people moving beyond limited ways of seeing themselves. These stories encourage us to remember, discover, or learn about our "true self" so that we can begin to find, create, and develop our potential.

We also benefit from reading old stories in a new way. For instance, an ancient tale tells about a woman who challenged a law that forbade eating fruit from a tree of knowledge. Instead of interpreting her action as wicked disobedience, we could see it as her way to escape from the garden of eternal childhood to find her own life and claim her own soul.

> Our life is a faint tracing on the surface of mystery.
> — ANNIE DILLARD, *PILGRIM AT TINKER CREEK*

Remembering our essential selves does not mean returning to the state of our original innocence and vulnerability. We do not go back to childhood, and we do not need to give up anything. Remembering simply gives us more choices, allowing us to join the unconscious intuition of childhood with the knowledge we have gained in our life's journey. This is often referred to as wisdom.

> One moment, the mountain is clear
> in strong morning sunlight. The next, vanished in fog.
> I return to Tu Fu, afraid to look up again
> from my reading and find in the window moonlight—
> but when I do, the fog is still there,
> and only the ancient poet's hair has turned gray
> while a single wild goose passed him, silently climbing.
> — JANE HIRSHFIELD, "THE MOUNTAIN"

The Sufis teach that the fall of humanity was the result of an amnesia that caused us to forget both our origins and our destiny. This loss of memory, they believe, is the true cause of our human troubles. Light is used as a metaphor to remind us of the inner self within. Every Friday night, the Shabbat candles are lit in Jewish homes the world over to help people remember and draw blessings from this light. It is always the woman who lights these candles.

From the almanac of last things
I choose the spider lily
for the grace of its brief
blossom, though I myself
fear brevity,

but I choose The Song of Songs
because the flesh
of those pomegranates
has survived
all the frost of dogma.

I choose January with its chill
lessons of patience and despair—and
August, too sun-struck for lessons.
I choose a thimbleful of red wine
to make my heart race,

then another to help me
sleep. From the almanac
of last things I choose you,
as I have done before.
And I choose evening

because the light clinging
to the window
is at its most reflective
just as it is ready
to go out.

— LINDA PASTAN, "THE ALMANAC OF LAST THINGS"

Reflection Questions

I was taken from my mother immediately after birth and did not see her again for nearly half a century. During those intervening years, I had a recurring dream of moving toward someone whose arms were extended to receive me, each of us slowly making their way to the other. Suddenly, a wall would rise up, or a platoon of soldiers would link arms between us, or the earth would crack open, and they would each drop away.

Forty-seven years later, I reunited with my mother, and we spent three days in San Francisco, the city where we had been separated so long ago. Together we visited the apartment where she had been pregnant with me. We sat down on the curb outside the grey Montgomery Street building and there my mother told me a story.

After my mother had given birth, she was placed in a ward with other new mothers. At feeding time, the babies were wheeled into the room. She reached out for me, and a nurse began to hand me to her. Suddenly a doctor appeared and stood between the nurse holding me and my eager mother with open arms. "Not her," he said, pointing to me. "Return her to the nursery!" That was the last time she saw me.

I have not had that dream again in all the years since my mother told me this story. In a way I still don't understand, my mind was able to let go of my fears as soon as I learned their origins.

— LINDA CARROLL

↪ What do you know about your mother's pregnancy and your birth? What do you imagine the experience was like for each of you?

↪ What was occurring in your parents' lives when you were born? Were they able to welcome you into the world?

↪ Think about your own experience of forgetting. How does forgetting continue to hinder your life today?

↪ What images or dreams reconnect you with early memories or with a sense of spirit and awakening?

> *Our life's journey is a circular one as we move from the unconscious intuition of childhood through knowledge and back to the intuitive perception, which is the wisdom of old age.*
>
> — SALLIE NICHOLS, *JUNG AND TAROT*

Chapter 4

Remembering

———◆———

Three Times My Life Has Opened
Three times my life has opened.
Once, into darkness and rain.
Once, into what the body carries at all times within
  it and starts
  to remember each time it enters the act of love.
Once, to the fire that holds all.
These three were not different.
You will recognize what I am saying or you will
  not.
But outside my window all day a maple has
  stepped from her leaves
  like a woman in love with winter, dropping the
  colored silks.
Neither are we different in what we know.
There is a door. It opens. Then it is closed. But a
  slip of light
  stays, like a scrap of unreadable paper left on

the floor,
or the one red leaf the snow releases in March
— JANE HIRSHFIELD, "THREE TIMES MY LIFE HAS OPENED"

Many of us are aware at some point of stepping through a doorway which changes how we view ourselves and our lives. It is a moment of seeing beyond the perspectives that previously held us. Once it has happened, nothing looks quite the same again. There is a Hindu story that refers to this as the "roar of awakening," the moment when we begin to realize that our identity is bigger and connected to a larger universe than we had known before. This is "Remembering."

Two girls discover
the secret of life
in a sudden line of
poetry.

I who don't know the
secret wrote
the line. They
told me

(through a third person)
they had found it
but not what it was,
not even

what line it was. No doubt
by now, more than a week
later, they have forgotten
the secret,

the line, the name of
the poem. I love them
for finding what
I can't find,

and for loving me
for the line I wrote:
and for forgetting it
so that

a thousand times, till death
finds them, they may
discover it again, in other
lines

in other
happenings. And for
wanting to know it,
for

assuming there is
such a secret, yes,
for that
most of all.

— DENISE LEVERTOV, "THE SECRET"

We Westerners use the term "self" to refer to everything about us that we see as unique—physical characteristics, preferences, personality traits, and our life story. Individuality is prized, and we form strong attachments to people and things with which we identify. Sometimes our attachments become addictions or obsessions.

"One day you're a peacock, the next a feather duster," says a familiar cliché, and it is so with the personality, which is most often caught in cycles of rising grandiosity or crashing deficiency. This waxing and waning of personal value is usually correlated with how we see ourselves in relationship to the world around us, which like a mirror reflects other people's judgments as though they were our own truths.

This is not the self we seek most of all. Our hunger is for the self that Judaism refers to as the "still, small voice within." This Self transcends gender, religion, culture, and family. It is at the center of our unifying wisdom, which Carl Jung defined as our "collective unconscious." The outer self is easier to see because it is in the world around us; glimpsing the inner and invisible self is more difficult, like looking for the source of a flashlight by observing the objects being illuminated. When we are lucky, though, we have experiences that allow us to see the light.

> I am the stone step,
> the latch, and the working hinge . . .
>
> I am the heart contracted by joy . . .
> the longest hair, white
> before the rest . . .
>
> I am there in the basket of fruit
> presented to the widow . . .
>
> I am the musk rose opening
> unattended, the fern on the boggy summit . . .
>
> I am the one whose love
> overcomes you, already with you
> when you think to call my name. . . .
> — JANE KENYON, "BRIEFLY IT ENTERS, AND BRIEFLY SPEAKS"

These are the moments we refer to as remembering what we are most truly connected to. Such experiences unexpectedly and open new doorways. We may turn away from what we see. Or understanding might grow on us.

> Look how our darkness is made true by light!
> Look how our silence is confirmed by birds!
> The mind that pastured ankle-deep in flowers
> Last night, must wake to sunrise on the river,
> Graze wide and then grow vertical as mountains;

For even a glimpse of mountains fogged with rain
Or mirrored in a river brings delight
And shakes us all as dawn shakes birds and flowers.
— JANE COOPER, FROM "MORNING ON THE ST. JOHN'S"

We find clues to our deeper self scattered throughout our childhood in obvious or obscure ways. A therapist once said that her earliest report cards were filled with complaints from her teachers. "Always talking to her friends" was one criticism. "She shouldn't be in other people's business so much" was another. Now, almost forty years later, she continues to be as fascinated with people's stories as she was when she began her career. And she recognizes that her greatest professional gifts were evident as a child, masked as problems to be overcome.

Sometimes a "wake-up call" occurs in an altered state. The novelist Virginia Woolf describes such an experience in her autobiography, *A Sketch of the Past*:

> *If life has a base that it stands upon; if it is a bowl that one fills and fills and fills—then my bowl without a doubt stands upon this memory. It is of lying half asleep, half awake, in bed in the nursery at St. Ives. It is of hearing the waves breaking, one, two, one, two, and sending a splash of water over the beach; and then breaking, one, two, one, two, behind a yellow blind. It is of hearing the blind draw its little acorn across the floor as the wind blows the blind out. It is of lying and hearing this splash and seeing this light, and feeling, it is almost impossible that I should be here; of feeling the purest ecstasy I can conceive.*

Woolf's experience occurred in a dreamy state: a nonverbal and imaginative realm. This is the place of dreams, intuition, and what is sometimes called the sixth sense.

> *Remember that you are this universe and that this*
> *universe is you.*
> *Remember that all is in motion, is growing, is you.*

Remember that language comes from this.
Remember the dance that language is, that life is.
Remember.

— JOY HARJO, "REMEMBER"

Western culture does not attach much significance to dream states. When young children speak of seeing bears, angels, or visiting magical realms, adults often discount these visions as "imaginary."

Many cultures believe each experience of consciousness is valuable. Australian aborigines and the African Dogons honor dreamtime wisdom more than the thoughts that crowd ordinary reality. To the Cuna Indians of Panama, dreams are considered omens for the day and announced publicly at village meetings. Such traditions allow the spiritual to enter their lives through the doorways of intuition and dream states.

At Sixteen I believed the moonlight
could change me if it would.

I moved my head
on the pillow, even moved my bed
as the moon slowly
crossed the open lattice.

I wanted beauty, a dangerous
gleam of steel, my body thinner,
my face paler.
I moonbathed
diligently, as others sunbathe.
But the moon's unsmiling stare
kept me awake. Mornings,
I was flushed and cross.

It was on dark nights of deep sleep
that I dreamed the most, sunk in the well,

and woke rested, and if not beautiful,
filled with some other power.
— DENISE LEVERTOV, "THE WELL"

The qualities of remembering run through our lives like golden threads, reminding us that we are more than our stories, more than the parts that make us smile with pleasure and greater than those that make us weep with despair.

We may experience its reflection at times of great loss. When I worked as a hospice counselor, I went to check on a woman, who had, just weeks before, lost her husband of fifty years after a long and difficult illness. She greeted me warmly and invited me into her home. When I began to express my condolences, the widow interrupted me, saying, "Oh no, it wasn't the way you think. Would you like to see photos?"

I tried to hide my surprise as I looked through the photographs. Page after page showed a man ravaged by cancer, as he proceeded from sick bed to coffin. As the widow showed me the pictures, she spoke with wonder about the time of his death, until at last it became clear that she was seeing something in those photographs I did not. Later, as I sat with others who were dying, I began to understand that sometimes, at such moments, something else fills the room; palpable, luminous, it bestows a blessing on those who are present.

A certain day became a presence to me;
there it was, confronting me—a sky, air light:
a being. And before it started to descend
from the height of noon, it leaned over
and struck my shoulder as if with
the flat of a sword, granting me
honor and a task. The day's blow
rang out, metallic—or it was I, a bell awakened,
and what I heard was my whole self
saying and singing what it knew: I can.
— DENISE LEVERTOV, "VARIATIONS ON A THEME BY RILKE"

Rhythms of life fill our universe. Tides of the ocean, cycles of the moon, plants that go from seeding to sprouting to bursting and then back to seed are a part of this rhythmic flow. The Old Testament reminds us: "to everything there is a season, and a time to every purpose unto heaven."

As we navigate through these seasons, we reflect on our experiences and their meaning. It is self-reflection that allows us to create art, to write, to mentor, and to ponder. The season of remembering speaks to a deeper place inside us.

It was taken some time ago.
At first it seems to be
a smeared
print: blurred lines and grey flecks
blended with the paper;

then, as you scan
it, you see in the left-hand corner
a thing that is like a branch: part of a tree
(balsam or spruce) emerging
and, to the right, halfway up
what ought to be a gentle
slope, a small frame house.

In the background there is a lake,
and beyond that, some low hills.

(The photograph was taken
the day after I drowned.

I am in the lake, in the center
of the picture, just under the surface.

It is difficult to say where
precisely, or to say
how large or small I am:

the effect of water
on light is a distortion

but if you look long enough,
eventually
you will be able to see me.)
— MARGARET ATWOOD, "THIS IS A PHOTOGRAPH OF ME"

What this writer is describing is not explained by biography, ancestry, or education. It is separated from our waking life by a very thin veil. Sometimes we remember without effort what is behind this curtain. Other times we have to work hard to shine a light into this place. Whenever we do recognize it, however, our lives brighten and our possibilities expand in immense and unimaginable ways.

One of the great social consciences of an era, Dorothy Day, led a life in which social activism and religious conviction became indivisible. Day remembers her spiritual awakening as a seven- or eight-year-old girl:

I'm sitting with my mother, and she's telling me about some trouble in the world, about children like me who don't have enough food— they're dying. I'm eating a doughnut. . . . I remember trying to understand what it meant—me eating a doughnut, and lots of children with no food at all. Finally, I must have decided to solve the world's problem of hunger on my own.

This thought was the messenger, to nudge Day toward her life's work. Such moments offer us threads to the soul's distinctive gifts.

True self-understanding requires we tap into the realm of soul. To join body, mind, and spirit, trekking into nature can be the best ground to find answers. Sometimes in the most painful moments of life, photographs, poetry, or the rustle of leaves provide the greatest comfort.

When loving friends an offering brought,
The first flowers of the year,

Culled from the precincts of our home,
From nooks to memory dear,
With some sad thoughts the work was done,
Unprompted and unbidden,
But joy it brought to my hidden life,
To consciousness no longer hidden.
I felt a power unfelt before,
Controlling weakness, languor, pain;
It bore me to the terrace-walk
I trod the hills again.
No prisoner in this lonely room,
I saw the green banks of the Wye
Recalling thy prophetic words—
Bard, brother, friend from infancy!
No need of motion or of strength
Or even breathing air,
I thought of nature's loveliest scenes,
And with memory I was there.

— DOROTHY WORDSWORTH, "THOUGHTS ON MY SICKBED"

The individualized self, often referred to as the "ego," seeks experience, seeks accomplishments, and is filled with questions of why, who, and how. This self defends, justifies, figures, and plans. It develops strategies and skills. It speaks to us through logic, desires, and instincts.

The spiritual Self is simpler, quiet and certain. It does not lament about the past or worry about what lies ahead, it is only concerned with the present moment. It speaks to us from within our bodies. It encourages us to wake up to what has true heart and meaning in our lives.

"The Kingdom of God does
not come if you watch for it.
Nor will anyone be able to say,
'It is here,'
or

'it is there,'
For the Kingdom of God is within you."
— JESUS OF NAZARETH

Most principles that guide people's religious lives originated in extraordinary states of Remembering passed on by prophets. The Buddha woke up under the Bodhi tree. From his meditation, he brought the world a message. "Stay awake," he said, and the power of his message has been passed through the centuries.

On Such a Day
Some hang above the tombs,
Some weep in empty rooms,
I, when the iris blooms,
   Remember

I, when the cyclamen
Opens her buds again,
Rejoice a moment—then
   Remember
  — MARY ELIZABETH COLERIDGE

Reflection Questions

When I was five years old, I had my first recognition of God. I was sitting on the curb in front of my home, feeding sugar to ants. I watched with fascination as they marched back and forth, wondering at their strange little bodies moving in straight lines. The thought came in an instant: "I know a world the ants know nothing about."

More startling still was the idea that followed. At the very moment that I was watching the ants, maybe something—or someone—was watching me. In that moment, my understanding of life changed, as though I had stepped through a doorway into an unknown world. My *senses grew keener, the bees buzzed louder, the white daisies looked brighter.*

Soon the acute sensory experience faded, my heartbeat slowed, and life appeared to return to normal. Yet a profound change had taken place. I was now aware of the two worlds I lived in, an outer one I showed to others and a private, inner one filled with wonder.

− LINDA CARROLL

↪ Can you remember being in a dream state when you were a child, asleep or in a lucid state?

↪ What was the message you heard about "daydreaming" when you were younger? Do you daydream today? About what? Do you have any judgments about the value of your daydreams?

↪ What is a story of remembrance and awakening you've experienced? Reflect on its current meaning in your life.

Chapter 5

Exploring

——⊶——

there is an amazon in us
She is the secret we do not
have to learn
the strength that opens us
beyond ourselves.
Birth is our birthright
We smile our mysterious smile.
— LUCILLE CLIFTON, "FEMALE"

At the age of forty-three, I awoke with a start in the middle of the night and realized that one day I was going to die. Of course, I had always known this, but knowing it was far different from feeling it in my belly. This time the realization registered deep inside, and what I understood was stunning. One day, my body would stop breathing, my remains would be disposed of, and the "I" to whom I was so attached, with all its loves and personal dramas, would die, too. Time in my life, I thought, was running out.

The sun rose the next morning, as on any other day, but to me everything seemed different. What had happened the night before had changed me, leaving me with a strong sense of urgency to examine my life and who I was more deeply than I ever had.

The urge to explore can arise out of something other than facing your mortality at four o'clock in the morning. You may have had an experience that your belief system cannot explain. Perhaps a great loss—or even a string of achievements—has left you feeling empty. Or a new possibility has opened for you, and you find yourself curious to consider an idea that you were once resistant to.

Before you know what kindness really is
you must lose things,
feel the future dissolve in a moment
like salt in a weakened broth.
What you held in your hand,
what you counted and carefully saved,
all this must go so you know
how desolate the landscape can be
between the regions of kindness.
How you ride and ride
thinking the bus will never stop,
the passengers eating maize and chicken
will stare out the window forever.

Before you learn the tender gravity of
kindness,
you must travel where the Indian in a white poncho
lies dead by the side of the road.
You must see how this could be you,
how he too was someone
who journeyed through the night with plans
and the simple breath that kept him alive.

Before you know kindness as the deepest thing inside,
you must know sorrow as the other deepest thing.
You must wake up with sorrow.
You must speak to it till your voice
catches the thread of all sorrows
and you see the size of the cloth.

Then it is only kindness that makes sense anymore,
only kindness that ties your shoes
and sends you out into the day to mail letters and
purchase bread,
only kindness that raises its head
from the crowd of the world to say
it is I you have been looking for,
and then goes with you everywhere
like a shadow or a friend.
— NAOMI SHIHAB NYE, "KINDNESS"

A time may come, too, when the lights go out within. What we have held dear and most essential loses its meaning. We are empty, and the ground trembles as in an earthquake. We compensate by filling our emptiness with *more*: bigger ego, bigger fame, more success; more buildings, more babies; more getting and spending. Or we try to fill the vacuum with *new*: a new and improved soul mate or lover, new places to vacation, new activities. Alcohol or drugs may fill the void, at least temporarily. Then the stage called Exploring may take on new and even desperate meanings.

These ways of exploring ultimately carry us further from our essential selves. But there are other ways of exploring that carry us closer.

The great trick to experiencing wholeness is to let go of the illusion that any of us is either superior or inferior and to fully allow ourselves to be who we are—our gender, our culture, our individual selves— without that preventing us from learning from and incorporating the wisdom of others.

This is the heroic challenge before humanity today . . . allowing cross-fertilization of these many traditions and wisdoms so that their synergy will produce something even greater than what came before.
— CAROL S. PEARSON, *AWAKENING THE HEROES WITHIN*

Journey to a Sacred Place

People have always traveled for spiritual purposes, their pilgrimages taking them on an inner journey even as they move toward a sacred place in the world. Christians journey to Bethlehem, Catholics to Rome, and Hindus to the Ganges. Muslims hope to travel at least once in their lifetime to Mecca. Jews return to Israel and Buddhists to the Bodhi Tree in India. People who do not belong to an organized religion also travel to tall mountains and sacred sites to find their own definition of spirit. Machu Picchu in Peru, Delphi in Greece, and Mt. McKinley in Denali Park are among those places we think of as sacred places filled with soul.

Travel is also metaphorical, signaling an opportunity to see our lives and ourselves anew. The French novelist Colette anticipated such renewal as a consequence of a "journey" she was about to take with a new lover:

I am going away with him to an unknown country where I shall have no past and no name, and where I shall be born again with a new face and an untried heart.

The poet Margaret Ronda marvels at how personal effects in a hotel room convey the durability of self:

Tomorrow this room will be emptied of all my traces. All the blonde hairs swept away, the ashtrays emptied, the bed sheets changed and refolded. Tonight, packing, each object comforts me with its solidity, its reassurance that I am a durable self. This wooden hairbrush, chapstick, soap, scarf, matchbox, black dress—what pleasure I take

in their material presence. How admirably they fulfill their function!
At home, cluttering a house crammed with other objects, they lose
their singularity. Here, they retain their domestic traces, remind me
of that other world I inhabit.

We travel to forget, to be reminded, to risk, and to recover. We
go to a place that is unfamiliar to break the spell, to stop living in
a trance. From a distance, away from daily habits and rituals, we
are able to see the filters we have used in defining ourselves. These
filters do not change the scene; they change our perception of the
view. Colette sees an opportunity to experience herself in a new way;
Ronda notices the ordinary items of daily life through a different
outlook. This is the kind of exploration in which we'll meet both the
sacred and the ordinary and find, at times, they are the same.

Watching the moon
at midnight
solitary, mid-sky,
I knew myself completely,
no part left out.
— IZUMI SHIKIBU

Separating the Wheat from the Chaff

Often women begin their adult spiritual journey by going deeper
into the faith they grew up in. Other women find the religion of their
childhood has been a source of pain or no longer nourishes them.
Many feel we were introduced to God as a male figure and received
our religious instruction within a patriarchal structure.

Over the past several decades, however, we have begun to see
the cost both to men and women of centuries of bondage to this
system. Both genders are adversely affected by cultural messages that
denigrate the feminine, and some carry the wounds of abuse. Unfortunately, these messages exist unapologetically in many forms of

mainstream religions, as Denise Carmody points out in *Women and World Religions*:

> *Buddhist women could not head the religious community. Hinduism usually held women ineligible for salvation. Islam made a woman's witness only half that of a man. Christianity called women the weaker vessel, the more blurred image of the Image. Jewish men blessed God for not having made them a woman.*

What these traditions share is ambivalence about a woman's strengths. On the one hand, her body is the source of life and thus is to be venerated. On the other, her body exudes sexual power and thus must be treated with caution, sometimes with fear, and even hostility. To make our way within these traditions, Carmody suggests, women first have to separate the "sexist chaff" from the "wheat of authentic religion." If we don't make such distinctions, we are liable to be split as well. Our bodies may be where we live, but many of us are not really at home.

Finding safe and nurturing ways to explore our sexuality, both historically and personally, is essential to self-discovery. Body therapies as well as dancing, walking, hiking, and martial arts are some ways you can live more fully in your body. Enhancing the sensual—smell, taste, touch, sight, and sound—is another way to explore the wonders of the physical. Exploring your place on earth and your purpose for being here most often begins by becoming more comfortable in your own skin—the house in which you live.

> *I can worship*
> *You*
> *But I cannot give*
> *You everything.*
>
> *If you cannot*
> *Adore*

This body.
If you cannot
Put your lips
To my
Clear water.
If you cannot
Rub bellies
With
My sun.
— ALICE WALKER, "I CAN WORSHIP YOU"

Different Paths

We spend more time thinking than anything else, often recycling the same thoughts and beliefs. Yet there are other truths beyond these everyday patterns of thought. As the Sufi poet Rumi said:

Out beyond ideas of right doing and wrong doing there is a field. I'll meet you there.

On that field are ideas that may be new to you: reincarnation, astrology, Zen meditation, and the rich possibility of other maps of consciousness, such as Tarot and the I Ching and the chakra system. These maps chart universal principles of ethical and human development, and they can be read as commentary on your own life. It's not a matter of believing or not believing in these ways of reading the world. Instead, it is more fruitful to look at them as different paths of exploration toward a single end.

We can learn much about exploration by turning to people who have gone before us. Instructors come in many forms. The obvious ones include ministers, rabbis, priests, gurus, shamans, elders, rabbis, and sometimes therapists. But there are also teachers who are not so obvious. In her series of books about a woman's experience of shamanism, Lynn Andrews refers frequently to "Red Dog," a wicked sorcerer who causes mischief and mishap to befall the story's heroine. But as Andrews wisely shows, the person who rubs us the wrong way, or whom we feel has been put here just for the purpose of tormenting us, often brings us our most important lessons.

Opportunities abound to retreat from the crowd, stop the outside chatter, and hear our inner voices. For centuries, ashrams, monasteries, and temples have been refuges for seekers of spirit. Today, retreats, workshops, seminars, and groups of women coming together offer safely guided processes to enhance our powers of intuition and creativity and release old emotional blocks. Dream work and guided imagery, fasting, and Holotropic Breathwork™ techniques are a few possibilities. Massage, dance, and qigong are other tools for internal focus. This is the place where we will ultimately find the clarity we seek.

I was passionate
filled with longing,
I searched
far and wide

but the day
that the Truthful One
found me
I was at home.

— LAL DED, FOURTEENTH CENTURY POETESS SAINT

The Harvest

A "wake-up call" is a cliché. It describes a moment that shakes us out of the self we take for granted, shakes us momentarily free of unquestioned assumptions and sends us on a journey of change. The call can come gently when we read a book, observe a flock of wild geese heading south, or see the first peonies of spring.

White peonies blooming along the porch
send out light
while the rest of the yard grows dim.

Outrageous flowers as big as human
heads! They're staggered
by their own luxuriance: I had
to prop them up with stakes and twine.
The moist air intensifies their scent,
and the moon moves around the barn
to find out what it's coming from.

In the darkening June evening
I draw a blossom near, and bending close
search it as a woman searches
a loved one's face.
— JANE KENYON, "PEONIES AT DUSK"

It can be more dramatic. Like Dorothy of Oz, we may be wrenched from our all-too-familiar world by a tornado, illness, a divorce, or even when we wake from a sinister dream, heart pounding.

Even such egregious events as abuse from a parent may look different when we can imagine the offending parent as a small child with his own pain and injustice to contend with, as Sharon Olds describes so powerfully in "Late Poem to My Father."

Suddenly I thought of you
as a child in that house, the unlit rooms
and the hot fireplace with the man in front of it,
silent. You moved through the heavy air
in your physical beauty, a boy of seven,
helpless, smart, there were things the man
did near you, and he was your father,
the mold by which you were made. Down in the

cellar, the barrels of sweet apples,
picked at their peak from the tree, rotted and
rotted, and past the cellar door
the creek ran and ran, and something was
not given to you, or something was
taken from you that you were born with, so that
even at 30 and 40 you set the
oily medicine to your lips
every night, the poison to help you
drop down unconscious. I always thought the
point was what you did to us
as a grown man, but then I remembered that
child being formed in front of the fire, the
tiny bones inside his soul
twisted in greenstick fractures, the small
tendons that hold the heart in place
snapped. And what they did to you
you did not do to me. When I love you now,
I like to think I am giving my love
Directly to that boy in the fiery room,

As if it could reach him in time.

Whether realization comes from a nudge, a shove, or a violent wind, we are seeing a new aspect of ourselves. At first, we may be fearful of exploring further because this new view challenges any certainty of our judgments of how things and people are. Once we begin to recognize that there are many more ways than we imagined to see and understand the same event, there is no turning back from that awareness.

Reflection Questions

I discovered that by running against the wind with a bunch of pine branches in your hand you could have the pine trees singing right in your ears. . . .
— GEORGIA O'KEEFFE

➝ What have been the avenues of spiritual exploration you have found most helpful in the past?

➝ Have you ever participated in a women's group whose focus is exploration? What are your thoughts and feelings about doing so?

➝ What is your current focus of Exploring? What are the paths that you are drawn to, and which do you feel critical of or closed to? Might those also be a source of exploration, especially your resistance to learning about something new?

Chapter 6

Practicing

—◦∞◦—

The novelist Paula Fox has been writing for fifty years. When I asked her how she continues to find inspiration, she immediately quoted Robert Frost: "We dance round in a ring and suppose. But the Secret sits in the middle and knows."

"I dance around the ring," she repeated. "I go into the workroom, and there is the keyboard, and there is the paper. The effort I make is banal and humdrum. Then something happens. Part of me begins to think in a way I don't understand. It's as though all I do is make a place where the inspiration can land."

"Who writes your books, then?"

"Exactly," she replied.

Creating a spiritual life is something like writing a story. Ultimately, it's a mystery, one that will not happen unless you go into the workroom and make an effort, however banal and humdrum. In other words, you have to practice.

In the spring twilight
the full moon is shining:
Girls take their places
as though around an altar

Tell everyone
now, today, I shall
sing beautifully for
my friends' pleasure
— SAPPHO

All spiritual traditions incorporate ways to do this: attending services and participating in religious rituals such as ablutions, chanting, and prayers. Some practices involve performing in a regular, consistent physical exercise, such as yoga, tai chi, and the martial arts.

Many women find great spiritual value in walking regularly, especially when accompanied by positive affirmations, mental imagery, and breath control techniques. Walking for mindfulness is not the same as walking for fitness, although you can do both at the same time.

Mindfulness is a word that comes up in Buddhist teachings and is associated with developing the "witness" self. In practicing mindfulness, you observe your thoughts and feelings in a nonjudgmental way. Sometimes you label the feelings, which serves to remind you that you are not the same as what you are watching. For instance, you might say, "I notice I am feeling angry," or "I see my thoughts are constantly going back to what happened at work." Mindfulness can be practiced in everyday activities such as eating. As you pay attention to yourself chewing and experiencing the texture, taste, and smell of the food, you are witnessing the process we usually ignore. Through this simple practice, you can enhance your ability to live the present moment.

In addition to witnessing, mindfulness lets us engage in what is sometimes called "inquiry." Here, we stand outside our feelings and thoughts and observe them instead of judging, analyzing, or denying them. This practice allows us to become less attached to our dramas, less victimized by our moods, and more aware of what is driving us.

A committed relationship is another form of practice. Oh, that's too easy, you may think. Many of us think of love as something that should be effortless and constant, something hardly in need of serious hard work. The poet Rainer Maria Rilke did not agree:

> To love is good, too: love being difficult. For one human being to love another; that is perhaps the most difficult of all our tasks, the ultimate, the last test and proof, the work for which all other work is but preparation.
>
> — RAINER MARIA RILKE, FROM *LETTERS TO A YOUNG POET*

The inevitable struggles and disappointments that are a normal part of relationships can help partners develop acceptance, honesty, flexibility, empathy, patience, and self-awareness. To do so, though, we must move off the path toward happiness and get on the one headed toward awakening. Ironically, when we relinquish the requirement that our partner be the source of our well-being, the relationship can become a wellspring of sustenance and nourishment.

Some teachings suggest that life itself, like relationships, is a practice. Ordinary challenges—growing a garden, raising children, or working a job—can be invitations to soul-work. Our daily lives offer us constant opportunities to increase appreciation, compassion, and selflessness.

> Does God have a set way of prayer, a way that He expects each of us to follow? I doubt it. I believe some people—lots of people—pray through the witness of their lives, through the work they do, the friendship they have, the love they offer people and receive from people. Since when are words the only acceptable form of prayer?
>
> — DOROTHY DAY

Teacher and anthropologist Angeles Arrien teaches people how to "walk the mystical path with practical feet," because to be effective in our lives, we need to do both. Angeles designed The Four-Fold Way as an educational program based around four principles that integrate "ancient cultural wisdoms into contemporary life."

The Four-Fold Way

1. Show up, be present.
2. Pay attention to what has heart and meaning.
3. Tell the truth without blame or judgment.
4. Be open to, but not attached to, outcome.

Show Up, Be Present

Once we have committed ourselves to spiritual practice, the first thing we must do is follow through with action.

Practicing is about showing up! Practice is doing your chosen technique, saying your selected prayer, writing in your journal each morning or performing your daily ritual even when you are bored, uninspired, defeated, when you wish you had never begun this practice, when you do not believe in it, when you are disgusted with it all.

> I love people who harness themselves, an ox to a heavy cart,
> who pull like water buffalo, with massive patience,
> who strain in the mud and the muck to move things forward,
> who do what has to be done, again and again.
> — MARGE PIERCY, "TO BE OF USE"

Many religions set aside a day each week for people to practice their faith. There are designated times during the year for fasting, praying, and reading scripture. Muslims bow in prayer five times a day. The Balinese Hindus offer baskets filled with flowers and rice to their deities every morning, afternoon, and evening, and the Benedictine nuns sing daily Gregonian chants. Establish a schedule for your own practice—it doesn't have to be perfect, it doesn't have to make you happy—but make it good enough to get you to show up and stay grounded. Mysticism causes us to soar; showing up keeps us rooted to the earth.

I attended a ten-day meditation retreat in the Berkshire Mountains in Massachusetts. By the last day of this event, the sense of calm was so strong among those gathered there that I wondered if our serenity had permeated the consciousness of the world at large. After the retreat was over, I took a train to meet my fourteen-year-old daughter in New York City. As I rolled along through the countryside, I noticed colors were brighter, people were friendlier, and my openness to life felt palpable.

At Grand Central Station, just as I embraced my daughter, a man came up alongside me and offered to carry my luggage. I smiled at him, taking his kind offer as evidence of the much hoped for planetary change of consciousness. He picked up my two suitcases and took off running through the station. I stood by helplessly as my daughter chased him down. Returning with suitcases in hand, my daughter asked, "Mom, where is your head?"

To integrate spiritual practice with daily life, we must live in two worlds at once. If our heads are in the clouds, our feet must be planted enough in the world so that we don't place ourselves in danger.

I cannot dance, O Lord,
Unless you lead me.
If you wish me to leap joyfully,
Let me see You dance and sing—

Then I will leap into Love—
And from Love into Knowledge,
And from Knowledge into the Harvest,
That sweetest Fruit beyond human sense,

There I will stay with You, whirling.
— MECHTILD OF MAGDEBURG

Pay Attention to What Has Heart and Meaning

Becoming spiritually literate is about paying attention to what is in front of your eyes at each moment. Thinking about what was, or what could be, diminishes what is happening right now. If we do not pay attention to now, we may never recognize our true prayer or song, the connection to the spark we seek.

When we pay attention, we may be surprised.

Why didn't I see this before? —That my creative life is my deepest prayer. That I must pray it from my heart, from my soul. Not from my head or my need for security or approval or to gain some sort of repute. —So my thread is spinning new courses. And my thread, like my dreams, never lies, never leads me astray. Still I cannot stop thinking how brave I will have to be to follow it.

— SUE MONK KIDD, *THE DANCE OF THE DISSIDENT DAUGHTER*

Tell the Truth without Blame or Judgment

Truthfulness can be a weapon. To tell the truth to others, we must learn ways that are kind, clear, and give us the best chance of being heard. Telling the truth also means that we tell it to ourselves, even when it is painful to acknowledge.

The ninth step of the well-known Twelve-Step Program advises us to "make direct amends to people whenever possible, except when to do so would injure them or others." If we view honesty in the same way, we can reduce the chances of using truth-telling as a weapon. When we can speak without blame, people can often hear the truth in what we say.

Being nonjudgmental doesn't mean abandoning personal boundaries. It doesn't mean condoning or downplaying harm done, nor is it an alternative to justice or a substitute for amends. Being nonjudgmental may not even be a state we ever reach, but because of its healing properties, it is one we must continually strive for.

Be Open to, but Not Attached to, Outcome

When her sons were four and seven years old, Lily went to a spiritual retreat and made a recommitment to a meditation practice. When she returned home, she carefully set up an altar in the corner of her bedroom. She found a perfect candle of just the right color and a meditation cushion with Sanskrit phrases on it. Then she announced to the boys that she would be spending thirty minutes each day in her room meditating, during which time they needed to be very quiet.

The day she began her practice, they stood outside her room, compliant and quiet. After about ten minutes she heard a quiet buzzing, which began to increase decibel by decibel. She tried to ignore the sound, meditating with her special mantra, but the noise grew louder. Soon she could hear the boys pounding one another, quickly escalating into tears and yelling. In exasperation she jumped up, opened the door, and screamed at them, "You two better stop it right now. I mean STOP IT, damn it, I am doing my spiritual practice."

Her sons' faces fell at the sight of their raging mother, and Lily was struck by the absurdity of this scene. This was not the way it was supposed to be. Her practice was hurting all three of them. What her true practice should be, she realized, was to use every event in the day as an opportunity for kindness and patience to emerge. Nowhere was this practice more important than with her children.

There is a Buddhist saying attributed to Sengstan, the third Chinese Patriarch: "The great way is not difficult for those who have no preferences." But for those of us in the West, where fulfilling our every desire as quickly as possible is often called success, the great way is not so easy. Sometimes, though, it is what we would prefer least that brings us the greatest treasures.

Think back on the experiences that have made you the woman that you are—those painful incidents that taught you resilience, strength, and self-reliance. Would you have chosen to live through them if you had been writing the script? Probably none of us would. Sometimes it is the experiences we would never consciously choose that bring us the greatest treasures.

On our spiritual journey, we have been called out of the story of our lives to remember that we are something more. We have sought out books and teachings, discovered new sides to ourselves. Perhaps we have found a new community of people who support and understand our quest. The old life we were living before no longer fits us. The new life and self have not yet formed. Practice is the bridge that will take us there.

Reflection Questions

I believe that we learn by practice. Whether it means to learn to dance by practicing dancing or to learn to live by practicing living, the principles are the same. In each it is the performance of a dedicated precise set of acts, physical or intellectual, from which comes shape of achievement, a sense of one's being, and a satisfaction of spirit. One becomes in some area an athlete of God.

— MARTHA GRAHAM, *BLOOD MEMORY*

➝ What sabotages your efforts to change and grow?

➝ What practices do you do now? What practices would you like to do?

➝ What is the difference between intention and commitment in relationship to practicing?

Chapter 7

Shadows on the Path

————⋈————

There will be storms, child
There will be storms
And with each tempest
You will seem to stand alone
Against cruel winds

But with time, the rage and fury
Shall subside
And when the sky clears
You will find yourself
Clinging to someone
You would have never known
But for storms.
— MARGIE DEMERELL, "STORMS"

Glimpsing the possibilities that exist in our nature does not cause permanent spiritual enlightenment. Claiming the promise of that glimpse is a long and challenging passage. As we remember more of our truest nature, it is natural to question the existing structure of our lives. Integrating our new self-discoveries with the woman we thought we were is a process filled with losses, pitfalls, and new illusions, some of which are examined here.

> In the book of shadows
> the first page is dark
> and the second darker still,
> but on the next page,
> and the next, there is a flickering
> as if the shadows are dancing
> with the leaves they mimic.
> Before Narcissus found the pool
> it was his shadow he loved,
> the way we grow to love our deaths
> when we meet them
> in dreams. For as we turn
> the pages of the book
> each page grows heavier
> under our numbed fingers, and only
> the shadows themselves
> are weightless,
> only the shadows welcome us
> beneath their cool canopy.
> — LINDA PASTAN, "THE BOOK"

The Myth of Enlightenment

The illusion of enlightenment—a place of permanent arrival or an ultimate state of being—is one of the most common perils we are likely to experience as we move along our path. Buddhist students are warned about becoming attached to enlightenment as a goal. Many women do have moments of transcendence and see beyond the veil. The trick is not to dwell on the vision but to appreciate it as a glimpse of the divine as we move on to the work of living. Spirituality is not a goal; it is our essence. Depression, disillusionment, and doubt are a part of life. So are sorrow, anger, struggle for meaning, and difficulties with love. There is no escaping the human condition.

> *We are not human beings trying to be spiritual.*
> *We are spiritual beings trying to be human.*
> — JACQUELINE SMALL, TEACHER AND WRITER

A good teacher can help. Yet here, too, we must tread carefully. Misdeeds by teachers and masters are not infrequent, and power can often be abused. A guide who has not explored her own dark side or who is not open to challenge is not a safe person for a student to trust. Be open to doubt and question authority.

When I was eleven years old, I asked a priest if the stories in the Bible were true. The room fell silent. Thinking I ought to explain, I continued, "I mean all those pagan babies in Africa. Will they really go to hell?" I was immediately removed from the classroom and given a terrifying description of what would await me in the hereafter should I doubt Church teachings or ask such questions ever again.

Forty years later, as I stood on the banks of the Ganges River in India, a Sadhu with orange robes and a long beard approached me and asked if I wanted a blessing. Believing I need all the help I can get, I am usually open to gurus, amulets, and blessings of all kinds. When I said yes, the Sadhu removed a nasty-looking tin cup from under his robes and dipped it into the river. He told me that if I drank the water, it would make me strong and bring enlightenment.

I had spent three days looking at what was floating in those waters: dead cows, piles of garbage, and even human corpses. I looked at the cup, the man, and the river, and I could not drink. Still, I couldn't meet the Sadhu's eyes when I refused. Somewhere deep inside, that authoritative voice from childhood still shamed me.

The Secret Club

Reconnecting with our spiritual nature shortens the distance between us and the rest of the world. We begin to see we are only one
small part of a very large design. We gain in compassion and humility,
which may decrease our need to feel special. But sometimes the op-
posite occurs, and spirituality becomes like an exclusive country club.

In her book *God is No Laughing Matter* Julia Cameron gives us a
sense of this folly among what she calls "Very Spiritual People":

> *Sometimes when you talk to them, Very Spiritual People close their
> eyes and sort of nod sagely as if they were on heroin. They do this in
> lots of situations where they are being officially spiritual. You're at a
> spiritual talk, for example, or a concert, and all of a sudden, whoops,
> there go the eyes and now they're rocking back and forth a little in this
> kind of embarrassing way. Very spiritual people scare me to death.
> They know the secrets. It's like a spiritual clubhouse.*

Members of this clubhouse believe everything that happens can
be explained. Our thoughts in this life—or our actions in the last—
are at the root of our troubles. There may be some validity to this
idea, but our ability to comprehend the myriad causes of events is, at
best, limited. It is arrogant, for instance, to think we can really know
exactly why people get sick. Being spiritual does not give us total
immunity to illness. Many people live right and die young. You can
have positive thoughts and catch pneumonia or get cancer.

Cameron's observation that Very Spiritual People may act as
though they were on heroin is apt. Some people become addicted
to the highs of the spiritual journey. We have to be careful not to
be swept away, not to disengage from this world. When the Sufis say
"Trust God and tie your camel to a post," they are reminding us to stay
connected to both realities.

The first person I ever knew to have studied with a guru in
India was a woman who called herself "Shakti." Shakti sort of floated

when she walked. She wore brilliant-colored, filmy clothes and exotic bracelets and amulets of carved snakes and jaguars. She spoke frequently about "harmony," "manifestation," and "unconditional love" and honored the goddess in other women. In Shakti's presence, I always felt inadequate and ashamed of my lowly struggles with jealousy, resentment, and greed.

But after a while, I began to see a different part of her nature. I was surprised to hear how harshly Shakti judged people who were not vegetarians or who found meaning in traditional religions. I discovered that she was not able to maintain long-term relationships and had no contact with her family or friends from her past. Later she confided that her mother had abandoned the family when she was seven years old, leaving her and six siblings in the hands of an abusive, alcoholic father. I began to realize that Shakti had never dealt directly with the pain and anguish of her early experiences. Instead, she had taken a "spiritual bypass"; that is, she was using spirituality to hide her problems from herself. This led to self-righteousness and the pose of superiority.

Many people who have long been practicing a spiritual way of life do not act pious or feel superior, nor do they over-romanticize the spiritual journey. They are modest about their mystical experiences and daily practice, smile easily and are the first to laugh at their own human foibles.

The Doctrine of Dualism

We have the potential to claim more wholeness and peace of mind than we imagine. We also have egos, body personal dramas, instincts, and a variety of hardwired emotions. The relationship between the ineffable and material is complex and interwoven.

Women who have fled rigid religious backgrounds may find themselves trapped in the same black-and-white thinking when they take up some of the New Age teachings. This doctrine of dualism—that the universe operates under two opposing principles, one light (or good) the other dark (or bad)—is at the root of some of the worst atrocities humans have committed, and some of the greatest personal suffering as well. That's not to deny the two sides exist; yet we are better off if we acknowledge that both coexist inside us. Our realities are always more complex than our concepts allow us to see.

> *Once, when I was more discontent than I knew,*
> *Living among Vietnamese exiles in southern France,*
> *I spent an afternoon trying to free a butterfly*
> *Battering her yellow wings against a window*
> *In an old stone barn that had been turned into a zendo.*
> *Finally she trusted me and stood on my finger,*
> *Saving herself with her surrender and redeeming me.*
> *In open air, she flew away into the tall grass*
> *Where three tiger kittens with yellow eyes*
> *Played near the bamboo grove.*
> *One pounced and ate her*
> *And looked at me.*
> *Yellow eyes,*
> *So beautiful.*
> — KATY BUTLER, "DELIVERANCE"

The Spiritual Emergency

As we move beyond limiting views of reality, we gain greater access to our Essence, and eventually find ourselves standing on new ground. Sometimes, though, if a person sees too much too quickly, she might suffer what writer and teacher Christina Grof calls a "spiritual emergency," one she first had during childbirth:

> *As the people around me encouraged me to "push . . . push . . . nice and hard, [and] remember to breathe," I felt an abrupt snap somewhere inside of me as powerful and unfamiliar energies were released unexpectedly and began streaming through my body. I started to shake uncontrollably. Enormous electrical tremors coursed from my toes up my legs and spine to the top of my head. Brilliant*

mosaics of white light exploded in my head, and instead of continu-
ing the Lamaze panting, I felt strange, involuntary breathing rhythms
taking over. It was as though I had just been hit by some miraculous
but frightening force, and I was both excited and terrified. . . . As
soon as my son was delivered, I was given two shots of morphine,
which stopped the whole process.

The process reoccurred, however, during subsequent events in
her life—at the birth of her second child and in a near-fatal car
accident. On these occasions, Grof understood nothing about what
had happened to her. Worried about going insane, she became depressed and isolated. She went through a divorce and lost custody of
both her children. Only later did she learn that her experiences were
similar to those described by people doing consciousness work under
the direction of clinical researcher, Stanislaw Grof, whom she eventually married. As Christina learned, such mystical or peak experiences can be triggered not only by childbirth and trauma but also by
meditation, prayer, breathing techniques, fasting, sweat lodge rituals,
and through the use of psychotropic plants. She went on to found
The Spiritual Emergency Network.

The mental health profession in the United States is also beginning to understand that some of the characteristics of spiritual development can be confused with symptoms of mental illness. When
accurately understood, these characteristics are seen for what they
are—a part of the normal, potentially life-enhancing aspect of human development. The emergence of spiritual experience becomes
an emergency when not adequately supported, or more drastically,
when anesthetized away.

The Loss of Who We Have Been

Whether our spiritual evolution leads us to scale mystical peaks or
to settle into the repose of quiet new thoughts, eventually we reach

a point where our old life no longer works, and a new life has yet to take hold. Often an old story has to die before a new one can begin. This is the traditional training ground for healers and shamans. The heroine is invited to enter into a greater life by sacrificing her old way of living. But no matter how limiting the old way may be, shedding the familiar entails loss and death, at least metaphorically. Here, the path is filled with shadows.

> *i am running into a new year*
> *and the old years blow back*
> *like a wind*
> *that i catch in my hair*
> *like strong fingers like*
> *all my old promises and*
> *it will be hard to let go*
> *of what i said to myself*
> *about myself*
> *when i was sixteen and*
> *twenty-six and thirty-six but*
> *i am running into a new year and i beg what i love and*
> *i leave to forgive me*
> — LUCILLE CLIFTON, "I AM RUNNING INTO A NEW YEAR"

We may feel missionary zeal. Elation, excitement, and a certainty that we've found something precious may lead us to urge others, especially those we love, to adopt our point of view. We might find ourselves clumsily using words and phrases that don't begin to convey adequately our experience. When people respond with cynicism, or worse, when they merely humor us, we can feel pretty deflated. Spiritual discovery is a subjective experience; it cannot be told to another without sacrificing some of its magic.

On the other hand, inner change sometimes reveals itself in dramatic outward shifts in attitude and behavior. Rather than look at us blankly, the people in our lives may be critical, particularly if they feel threatened by the changes. We may mourn the loss of relationships with others, and sometimes grieve for the old self we have lost. We may sometimes regret that we ever began a spiritual search at all.

> *Do not think of her*
> *unless you are prepared*
> *to be driven to your limits,*
> *to rush forth from yourself*
> *like a ritual bowl overflowing*
> *with sacramental wine.*
>
> *Do not summon her image*
> *unless you are ready to be blinded,*
> *to stand in the flash*
> *of a center exploding,*
> *yourself shattering into the landscape,*
> *wavering bits of bark and water.*
>
> *Do not speak her name*
> *until you have said good-bye*
> *to all your familiar trinkets—*
> *your mirrors, your bracelets,*
> *your childhood adorations—*
> *From now on you are nothing,*
> *a ghost sighing at the window,*
> *a voice singing under water.*
>
> — DOROTHY WALTERS, "PREPARING TO GREET THE GODDESS"

Jung saw life as two phases. "Morning" is when we establish ourselves as adults and develop our competence in the outer world. "Afternoon" is the time for inner work, when the call of one's true nature gets louder, and always there are challenges and difficulties. Once so useful, old masks—protections, defenses, and ways of coping—may no longer fit. Taking them off may hurt, but keeping them on may hurt more. Near the end of her life, the late actress and comedienne Gilda Radner understood this. In her book *It's Always Something* she describes how she gave up the dream of perfect control and learned instead to embrace life in all its ragged uncertainty:

> *I wanted a perfect ending. Now I've learned, the hard way, that some poems don't rhyme, and some stories don't have a clear beginning, middle, and end. Life is about not knowing, having to change, taking the moment and making the best of it, without knowing what's going to happen next.*

Whatever wonders our journey shows us, we must remember that we are still human beings in the physical world. Cosmic moments of understanding come and go, and we plummet back into ordinary life. We cannot hold on, nor are we meant to. We may have been to the mountain and seen miracles, but we still need to do the laundry and remind our kids to brush their teeth.

Reflection Questions

> *The shadow side of community can be deadening conformity. The shadow side of empowerment can be arrogance. Passion can turn into fanaticism. And mystery without understanding can be kooky or terrorizing. Even the healing power of the spirit must be tempered with knowing when not to heal, for to relish life is to accept death.*
> — DEE BERRY

↝ Describe what have been the most difficult times in your journey in self-discovery and Spirit.

↝ What has been hardest in your relationships as you expand into your fullest potential?

↝ Think of three women from your life who would exemplify "pious." Now think of three women who seem to be deeply spiritual. What is similar about them; what is different?

Chapter 8

Reclaiming

———✼———

In 1974, a team of Russian mountain climbers composed entirely of women died in a storm on Lenin Peak. Their tragedy captivated the imagination of Adrienne Rich, the American poet, who wrote a tribute to the team's leader, Elvira Shatayev, entitled "Phantasia for Elvira Shatayev." Rich envisions the Russian leader's last hours as if she were inside Shatayev's mind. We face her fears, and feel her intense, driving love for her teammates. Rich's poem captures the climbers' desire for a truth that surpasses the everyday, a truth that is worth even the most extreme cost. These women explorers died in triumph, Rich persuades us, because they had arrived where they strove to be, transcending death by achieving a dream.

People of all cultures, past and present, tell stories about reaching great summits, whose heights are the site of spiritual enlightenment and self-discovery. They believe that the higher we go, the closer we get to the source of all spiritual life. In the past decade, the emergence of His Holiness the Dalai Lama as a world spiritual leader has focused attention on the Tibetan people, whose openheartedness is a source of inspiration for many of us. Tibetans have suffered unspeakable losses, yet they often display one of the truest signs of spiritual Reclaiming—a pervading sense of joy. Is it a coincidence that they live in the Himalayas, at some of the highest altitudes in the world?

Reclaiming is that stage in which we begin to recognize and trust those things that have meaning for us, and we take hold of the direction of our lives, both inside and out. It does not mean relinquishing your personality or giving up the ways you have learned to protect yourself. It means retrieving your intuition and inner resources and joining them with the wisdom and reason you have gained through living. Wisdom, joined with the heart and spirit, will help you remember why you are here, and how to make each moment count.

> Long ago on a night of danger and vigil
> a friend said, Why are you happy?
> He explained (we lay together
> on a hard cold floor) what prison
> meant because he had done
> time, and I talked of the death
> of friends. Why are you happy
> then, he asked, close to
> angry.
>
> I said, I like my life. If I
> have to give it back, if they
> take it from me, let me only
> not feel I wasted any, let me
> not feel I forgot to love anyone
> I meant to love, that I forgot
> to give what I held in my hands,
> that I forgot to do some little
> piece of the work that wanted
> to come through.
>
> Sun and moonshine, starshine,
> the muted grey light off the waters
> of the bay at night, the white
> light of the fog stealing in,

the first spears of the morning
touching a face
I love. We all lose
everything. We lose
ourselves. We are lost.

Only what we manage to do
lasts, what love sculpts from us;
but what I count, my rubies, my
children, are those moments
wide open when I know clearly
who I am, who you are, what we
do, a marigold, an oakleaf, a meteor,
with all my senses hungry and filled
at once like a pitcher with light.
— MARGE PIERCY, "IF THEY COME IN THE NIGHT"

Audre Lorde, in her poem "Black Mother Woman," describes the process of remembering the "true spirit" both of herself and her mother, as she "peels away" the surface layers of painful words and internalized anger to find the loving essence beneath:

I cannot recall you gentle.
Through your heavy love
I have become
an image of your once delicate flesh
split with deceitful longings.

When strangers come and compliment me
your aged spirit takes a bow
jingling with pride
but once you hid that secret
in the center of furies
hanging me
with deep breasts and wiry hair

with your own split flesh and long suffering eyes
buried in myths of no worth.

But I have peeled away your anger
down to its core of love
and look mother
I am   a dark temple
where your true spirit rises
beautiful and tough as a chestnut
stanchion against your nightmares of weakness
and if my eyes conceal
a squadron of conflicting rebellions
I learned from you
to define myself
through your denials.

Through reclaiming her own beauty and strength, Lorde's speaker comes to a new understanding of her mother's struggles. She turns away from this legacy of deception and self-denial to embrace her own "dark temple" with a new understanding.

Like Lorde, May Sarton describes a process of reclaiming that leads to a more fully realized sense of self:

Now I become myself. It's taken
Time, many years and places,
I have been dissolved and shaken,
Worn other people's faces,

Now to stand still, to be here,
Feel my own weight and density! . . .
Now there is time and Time is young.
O, in this single hour I live
All of myself and do not move
I, the pursued, who madly ran,
Stand still, stand still, and stop the Sun!
— MAY SORTON, "NOW I BECOME MYSELF"

Sometimes we reclaim our identity by discovering heroines to remind us that ordinary women, in an extraordinary moment, can make choices from their essence rather than from their usual way of responding.

Rosa Parks, tired from a long day's work, was told to give her seat to a white passenger on an Alabama bus in 1955. Tired of a life filled with people telling her what to do, tired from a long day at work and tired of accepting injustice, she simply said "no." That action marks a major landmark of the civil rights movement. Almost forty years later, after a robber attacked Parks in her own home, she demonstrated that strength had not mitigated her compassion. She wrote:

> I pray for this young man and the conditions in our country that have made him this way. Despite the violence and crime in our society, we should not let fear overwhelm us. We must remain strong.

Etty Hillesum, who died at the age of twenty-seven in Auschwitz, left behind an extraordinary diary in which she describes living from inner essence in spite of outer circumstances.

> One must keep in touch with the real world and know one's place in it; it is wrong to live only with the external truths, for then one is apt to end up behaving like an ostrich. To live fully, outwardly and inwardly, not to ignore external reality for the sake of the inner life, or the reverse—that's quite a task.

Burmese freedom fighter Daw Aung San Suu Kyi embodies her country's greatest hopes for democracy. Although confined in a dilapidated house and separated from her husband and sons for many years, she has never budged from her determination to bring political change to her country. Her book *Freedom From Fear* and a Nobel Peace Prize bear eloquent testimony to her unwavering spirit.

In the 1980s, Ukrainian mathematician Oksana Horbunova began to hear that Ukrainian women were being kidnapped for sale as sexual slaves, and that such trafficking was endemic in her country. She made it her life's mission to fight these crimes, bearing a multitude of threats as she personally escorted many victims back to their homes.

These women remind us how courage can coexist with compassion.

> When I look at my body I see a survivor. I am one-breasted—but I am more.
> I am more compassionate and open than I was before.
> — KRISTA GOTTLIEB

In reclaiming inner resources, we can turn to revered icons for solace and guidance. The Buddhist image of Kuan Yin sits on altars worldwide to remind us of compassion. According to legend, Kuan Yin paused at the threshold of heaven as she heard the cries of the world. She decided to stay and help humans, to give up heaven, the pinnacle of mercy and self-sacrifice.

Christian statues and pictures of Mary, mother of God, reveal the power of forgiveness and the miracle of love. The story of Mary's virgin birth of Jesus Christ reminds us that all things are possible with God. Although she was crowned "Queen of Heaven," she is said to remain close to her human children, comforting them with dreams and visions.

Hindu altars display contrasting symbols of the feminine. Some images are benevolent and gentle, others are malevolent and ferocious, but in all forms these goddesses represent the Mother from whom all life is born. For many Hindus, the most important goddess is Durga, the warrior deity who fights danger. Her face is a study of calm and serenity even as she slays the fiercest of dragons.

The female face of God appears worldwide in many forms to nourish, support, and remind women of their essential qualities.

When we reclaim who we are, when we begin to take back all of ourselves, the promise of our human and feminine spirituality emerges. We recover our personal history without the gloss of "perfect" or "happy," or the dark umbrella of "victim."

> It's all I have to bring today—
> This, and my heart beside—
> This, and my heart, and all the fields—
> And all the meadows wide—
> — EMILY DICKINSON

When we reclaim ourselves, we accept our bodies' strengths and limitations, whatever the wounds or flaws. We learn to eat well and exercise, yet forgive ourselves when we don't. We reclaim other aspects of our original selves: Our sensuality. Our sexuality. Our curiosity. Our sense of play. We may be more willing to experiment with life and to break the rules when we need to. We might relinquish obligations when they are outdated or harmful to us. We can learn to understand the meaning in our dreams, and we can trust this dream realm, finding new ways to draw strength and wisdom from it.

We will honor other women in a new and deeper way. Like many women before us, like Elvira Shatayev on her mountain climb, we will not let even the fiercest adversity stand in our way. And like Audre Lorde, we will discover new truths in our old stories.

Reflection Questions

> More and more I have come to admire resilience.
> Not the simple resistance of a pillow, whose foam
> returns over and over to the same shape, but the sinuous
> tenacity of a tree: finding the light newly blocked on one side,
> it turns in another. A blind intelligence, true.
> But out of such persistence arose turtles, rivers,
> mitochondria, figs—all this resinous, unretractable earth.
> — JANE HIRSHFIELD, "OPTIMISM"

↝ Give each woman a copy of "Phantasia for Elvira Shetayev" from Adrienne Rich's *The Dream of a Common Language*. As you read it together, ponder what it means in terms of women's friendship, camaraderie, and the issues of reclaiming.

↝ What are the points of attraction to you in your life today? What arouses your passion and energy? What in the current "story" of your life interests you? What helps you to listen to your own intuitive inner voice?

↝ Who are your heroines? Describe one who is living, and one from a spiritual tradition or a myth.

Chapter 9

Acceptance

—⭗—

Without words, it comes. And suddenly, sharply, one is aware of being separated from every person on one's earth and every object, and from the beginning of things and from the future and even a little, from one's self. A moment before one was happily playing, the world was round and friendly. Now at one's feet there are chasms that had been invisible until this moment.

— LILLIAN SMITH, *THE JOURNEY*

Our understanding of spirit becomes a river, deepening and widening. Our spiritual vision grows keener. We find ways to remember the golden cord we were born with, connecting us to the universe. We stand in two worlds more easily, the world of personality and the world of spirit. Like Dorothy in *The Wizard of Oz*, we look around with wonder at what has been in our lives all along.

The infinite a sudden Guest
Has been assumed to be—
But how can that stupendous come
Which never went away?
— EMILY DICKINSON

But our passage does not end when we remember our essential self any more than a relationship ends when one falls in love. Both experiences offer a grand promise and a roller coaster ride through trouble and possibilities. We will forget all we have learned, remember it, and forget it again. The deep hole of forgetting again is as much a part of our human experience as the breath we take.

Thus we enter the last stage of our journey, which is acceptance that moments of remembering don't last and change is inevitable. Each time a journey has ended, another one has begun. Life will throw us another challenge, the people we love will cause us pain, and our jobs will tire, bore, and frustrate us. Then we will recollect some of the places we have been spiritually, as though they were old photos in a travel album. We will find it hard to believe we ever felt so good, saw so much, or knew—even for an instant—a little piece of the truth.

We do not ride off into the sunset, like a heroine in an old-time movie. We trek through valleys and over peaks, experiencing many more dips and ascensions. We never finish searching, and the path we travel is a spiral, not a line. Changing ourselves is not just difficult; it can seem impossible at times. Our original protections and responses return frequently in times of stress, just when we believed they were gone. Resistance to change is a natural response; even as one part of us welcomes it, another part protests loudly.

I cannot walk an inch
without trying to walk to God.
I cannot move a finger
without trying to touch God.
Perhaps it is this way:

He is in the graves of the horses.
He is in the swarm, the frenzy of the bees,
He is in the tailor mending my pantsuit.
He is in Boston, raised up by the skyscrapers.
He is in the bird, that shameless flyer.
He is in the potter who makes clay into a kiss.

Heaven replies:
Not so! Not so!

I say thus and thus
and heaven smashes my words.

Is not God in the hiss of the river?

Not so! Not so!

Is not God in the ant heap,
stepping, clutching, dying, being born?

Not so! Not so!

Where then?
I cannot move an inch.

Look to your heart
that flutters in and out like a moth.
God is not indifferent to your need.
You have a thousand prayers
but God has one.
  — ANNE SEXTON, "NOT SO, NOT SO"

Like the metamorphosis of a butterfly, a true change of heart takes time. In our culture of instant gratification, marketing people sprinkle their advertising campaigns with words like "quick," "instant," and "easy." But there is no instant shortcut to spirituality. The writer May Sarton speaks of how difficult it is to accept our own slow blossoming, even though we expect it from the natural world:

> It does not astonish or make us angry that it takes a whole year to bring into the house three great white peonies, and two pale blue irises. It seems altogether right and appropriate that these glories are earned with long patience and faith, and also that it is altogether right and appropriate that they cannot last. Yet in our human relations we are outraged when the supreme moments, the moments of flowering, must be waited for . . . and then cannot last. We reach a summit and then have to go down again.

Acceptance of these difficulties, paradoxically, also illuminates the path better than anything else because it increases our tolerance for our human condition. And, although we sometimes forget the core of who we are, we remember more quickly than we once did. We grow more at home with the mystery of life, accepting that we can never pull the veil entirely aside and grasp the mystery of our lives. We develop our own understanding of what "spiritual" means. As its romantic connotations diminish, we appreciate the simplicity of a path that increases service, enlivens our creativity, deepens our ethics, and expands our compassion for all of life.

> Looking down into my father's
> dead face
> for the last time
> my mother said without
> tears, without smiles
> without regrets
> but with civility
> "Good night, Willie Lee, I'll see you
> in the morning."
> And it was then I knew that the healing
> of all our wounds

is forgiveness
that permits a promise
of our return
at the end.

— ALICE WALKER, "GOODNIGHT, WILLIE LEE, I'LL SEE YOU IN THE MORNING"

At this point in the journey, we realize we will forever be standing on new ground, and that change is the only certainty there is.

Things falling apart is a kind of testing and also a kind of healing. We think that the point is to pass the test or to overcome the problem, but the truth is that things don't really get solved. They come together and they fall apart. Then they come together again and fall apart again. It's just like that. The healing comes from letting there be room for all of this to happen: room for grief, for misery, for joy.

— PEMA CHÖDRÖN, *WHEN THINGS FALL APART: HEART ADVICE FOR DIFFICULT TIMES*

We will know what poet Lucille Clifton means when she writes: "The end of a thing is never the end. Something is always being born, like a year or a baby."

And so our journey begins again.

So few grains of happiness
measured against all the dark
and still the scales balance.

The world asks of us
only the strength we have and we give it.
Then it asks more, and we give it.

— JANE HIRSHFIELD, FROM "THE WEIGHING"

Reflection Questions

↪ What has shifted in your attitude as you follow a path of developing consciousness in your life journey?

↪ What is your current statement of "faith" regarding the nature of life and your own purpose?

Chapter 10

Using Remember Who You Are
in a Women's Group

—— ✧ ——

Reading *Remember Who You Are* may be undertaken as a solitary journey; however, it is rewarding to experience the stages through a women's group. Indeed, this process was developed through years of experience with women's circles, retreats, and group counseling. Exploring these steps in an ongoing women's circle, or beginning a new group utilizing the book as a focus, can be a powerful way to fully integrate these ideas into your life. *Remember Who You Are* has a spiritual emphasis, which makes room both for women who want to dive deeper into their own religious training and those who wish to define the sacred in a more eclectic way.

Studies have shown that involvement in a caring community enriches and extends one's life. A women's group can be just such a place, offering the support where we can touch our deepest selves and connect with others. Women's circles are often full of laughter, creative energy, challenging moments, joyful celebration, and intense feelings and thoughts. As a therapist, I have seen firsthand the ways that such groups can change people's lives. I encourage you to explore a women's group as an avenue for intensive self-exploration, new insight and a group of people to help us stay accountable to the changes we want to make in our lives.

Starting a Women's Group

The main criteria for creating a successful group are to find like-minded women with a shared sense of curiosity, a willingness to explore new or uncomfortable topics, and a desire for deeper knowledge of our essential selves.

In pulling a new group together, we can seek members by looking within our own circle of friends or any ongoing group we are a part of. Beyond that, we could inquire in local bookstores, church groups or reading groups for like-minded individuals. Many such places even have meeting rooms that are offered as a place to gather. Other possibilities include putting up a notice at a library or neighborhood coffee shop, or sending out an email to local listservs.

Having six to nine members allows sufficient time for each woman to participate, while also providing a rich variety of input. Fewer than six group members may feel too small if any woman is missing for the meeting. More than nine may make it difficult for each woman to have time to express herself.

A 12-week commitment, meeting each week for 2–3 hours, is a good way to begin your group. Though it may seem difficult to find sufficient time in one's schedule for a weekly meeting, the sense of continuity and intensity that such regular meetings make possible is ideal for the exploration of the questions.

If the group wishes to continue after this initial 12-week period, a recommitment on a 10–12 week basis can be negotiated. The members may wish at this time to change to a bimonthly meeting. The ideas and personal reflections generated by *Remember Who You Are* can provide an endless array of themes used in the meetings.

Ground Rules

Confidentiality is essential to creating a circle that is safe and strong. The group should talk about confidentiality at the first meeting, with each individual sharing what it means for her to make this agreement. What will be gained from honoring the commitment, and what is the cost if it is broken? Perhaps each woman can talk about a time when she told something that she had promised not to, or when somebody else shared something of hers that wasn't theirs to talk about. What did that feel like? What happened? What were the lessons in it?

It's important to remember people have different expectations about what confidentiality means. For one woman, it has to do with the vulnerabilities she is sharing. For another, it may mean that she doesn't want anyone to know she is attending such a group. For some women, it can include the promise that group members not discuss the group outside of the meetings. It is critical to establish shared expectations about what confidentiality entails for the group. This can prevent a painful situation later.

Commitment is just as important as confidentiality. When a member doesn't show up for a subsequent meeting, group members wait for her, wondering or worrying. It is important to let someone know if you will miss group or be late.

The group should be closed to new women after the second meeting. This helps bonds deepen and trust develop more fully.

Leadership

It is important to have someone in charge of each group meeting. The group may have one standing facilitator or have rotating leadership. Rotating leadership means that the group members take turns leading the meetings, setting the venue, managing the time, and opening and closing the circle.

As you set up the group, plan to have a candid discussion about leadership. Depending on the dynamics of the particular members involved, it may be easy or difficult to negotiate who will be responsible for facilitating the group. Make sure that everyone feels comfortable with the structure you are setting in place.

Being a leader of the meeting entails a particular sensitivity to the general climate of the room and the responses of each woman. At times, this can mean steering the conversation in a different direction or asking a difficult question. It is sometimes necessary for the leader to balance the talking time to ensure that each woman has a chance to be heard.

Whatever leadership form you decide to have, each woman shares responsibility for the overall success of the group.

Shared Responsibility

Shared responsibility means that each woman is responsible for managing herself in relation to the group. To achieve this, The Four Fold Plan, described in Chapter 6, is the best self-monitoring process I know:

- **Showing up** is about being there each week, making the commitment to the group a priority in your life, communicating with clarity, and responding appropriately to the others in the group.
- **Being present** includes the practice of listening, which includes paying attention to the other person without interruption, or co-opting her story for your own purposes. This also involves considering the impact of one's own words, and checking the impulse to fix others or to give uninvited feedback.
- **Tell the truth without blame or judgment** helps us remember that we are not there to evaluate or judge another person's experience. Staying authentic about our own experience is an important part of this step. A women's group is an important place to practice honesty, both with oneself and others, without being critical or hurtful.
- **Be open to but not attached to outcome** reminds us that we may receive unexpected gifts if we allow what is happening in the group to occur rather than trying to control it. This step asks

us to relinquish the desire to fully control our own experience, and the experiences of others in the group, and be alive to new discoveries.

Structure

Rituals draw each individual member more fully into the circle. Lighting a candle in the center reminds each woman that she comes to shed light on her own journey. A few minutes of silence, or a meditation, guided or with music, helps us to leave outside life at the door. It allows the mind time to slow down from its ongoing thoughts about the past or future, and to focus on the present.

The first meeting should be spent establishing the ways the group will work, talking about group format, duration, and shared leadership. Each member takes a turn sharing a little about herself, including expectations and reservations about being there. We usually have both when we join a group: we want something (connection, understanding, exploration), and we don't want something (the risk of sharing, commitment of time, fear of judgment).

The next several sessions should be spent going through each of the stages, beginning with the first chapter. Begin by answering the questions for reflection in the back of the chapter. Additional suggestions for working with each stage, and book titles on related themes, are included in the second part of this chapter. The suggested books can deepen exploration of the proposed materials. They can be read along with the chapter to facilitate group discussion, or be used in groups who wish to continue meeting after the initial sessions are completed. My suggested titles are to help you get started.

The final meeting should be a time for closure. Each woman should reflect on what the experience has meant to her, describing any challenges and gifts she has gained.

A Final Note

While women's groups offer a powerful model of community cohesion and deep self-exploration, they are not a replacement for the work one can do with a trained professional. If a woman is in the midst of a difficult transition, is experiencing a crisis, or is having intractable emotional issues, she should be undergoing counseling. The women's circle that *Remember Who You Are* advocates is intended for those who wish to deepen their self-understanding in a group context, rather than to deal with specific problems best handled in a therapeutic setting.

Recommended Reading

Sacred Circles: A Guide to Creating Your Own Women's Spirituality Group by Robin Deen Carnes and Sally Craig

Calling the Circle by Christina Baldwin

Urgent Message from Mother by Jean Shinoda Bolen

The Spiral Path: Explorations in Women's Spirituality by Theresa King

Using This Book:
Suggested Exercises and Related Book List

Chapter 1: The Golden Cord

Chapter 1 is about naming our essence. The suggested exercises for this chapter are to help us examine the meaning essence and to recognize our yearning for it. We must define it before we can set out to recapture it.

Suggestions:
- The facilitator poses the reflection questions at the end of Chapter 1. Women share their answers.
- The facilitator reads aloud the story about the woman in the window (page 17). Each woman writes a paragraph about what she believes the woman in the window is yearning for. The women take turns reading what they have written and look for common themes and differences.
- Each woman is encouraged to bring in and share poems that typify the chapter's ideas to her.
- The facilitator reads The Native American legend of the Golden Cord (page 19). The group discusses what they think the Golden Cord represents. Is it true?

Recommended Reading

The Feminine Face of God: The Unfolding of the Sacred in Women by Sherry Ruth Anderson

Women in Praise of the Sacred edited by Jane Hirshfield

Cries of the Spirit edited by Marilyn Sewell, Boston

Keys to the Open Gate by Kimberly Snow

The Human Odyssey by Thomas Armstrong

Chapter 2: The Human Search

Chapter 2 helps us to understand our common yearning to make meaning of our human experience. The suggested exercises are about new ways to approach and experience our humanness and searching for understanding.

Suggestions:

- The facilitator poses the reflection questions at the end of Chapter 2 (page 28). Women share their answers.
- Each woman reintroduces herself in this way:

  I am (name of woman), daughter of (name mother), granddaughter of (name grandmother).

  I received my name in this way. (Explains how her parents chose her name for her.)

This exercise reminds women of their continuing relationship to those who have come before. We remember the influence and potency of family, and examine the gifts family gives us and the ways our family cause us to forget our deeper selves.

- The evening's facilitator may bring in some meditations. Basic breath-guided meditations can be found online. They should focus on deep abdominal breathing, focusing attention on in-and-out breaths, counting breaths, watching the breath breathe you.
- The facilitator reads aloud the piece by A. K. Ramanujan, *Devara Dasimayyatr* (page 24). Women take turns discussing their reactions to the reading.
- The facilitator reads the Celtic tradition of *The Flower, The Fruit and, The Seed* (page 26). Women take turns discussing what stage they are in, what the previous stages were like, and what will come next for them. Where have they felt gifted or held hostage to their biology and stage of life?

Recommended Reading

The Dance of the Dissident Daughter: A Woman's Journey from Christian Tradition to the Sacred Feminine by Sue Monk Kidd

The Spiral Path: Explorations in Women's Spirituality by Theresa King

The Heroine's Journey by Maureen Murdock

Chapter 3: Forgetting

In forgetting our connection to our essence, we examine the masks that have kept us separated from both ourselves and others. The suggested exercises for this chapter are designed to help us understand the impact that our early life experience had on the creation of our masks. In a circle of women, we may help each other discover our true selves more easily than we can alone.

Suggestions:

The facilitator poses the reflection questions at the end of Chapter 3 (page 41). Women share their answers.

- Each woman can talk about her experience within her family of origin, describing her childhood, her particular gifts and struggles, her parents' relationship. The group might also explore their birth stories, examining what their parents and siblings told them about the day of their birth and the stories about their arrival.

- Using the "selves" described by Hal and Sidra Stone (page 36), each member of the group answers these questions: What do you know about your pleaser, critic, or protector? How did these "selves" emerge in you as a child? What did it mean to be a female in your childhood? What were the messages you got in relationship to your body, your mind, your emotions, and your spirit?

- Each woman can draw a picture of herself as a middle school girl. She shares it with the group and answers these questions: What did and didn't you like about the way you looked? What were some of the identities that you tried on as a girl? What did you learn about sexuality as an adolescent? What identities worked or didn't work?

- Maskmaking: "One day you're a peacock, the next a feather duster," becomes a theme for a night of making masks. Each woman makes a mask to illustrate how she looks when she is a peacock, riding high on the wings of grandiosity; another mask shows what it looks like to be a feather duster, sinking low on the downward spiral of deficiency.
- A final and essential set of questions to explore in a women's group: What was your peer experience with other girls? What did you learn from your mother about friendship? What do you feel about being a part of a group of women?

Recommended Reading

Storycatcher: Making Sense of Our Lives through the Power and Practice of Story by Christina Baldwin

Embracing Our Selves: The Voice Dialogue Manual by Hal and Sidra Stone

I Know Just What You Mean: The Power of Friendship in Women's Lives by Ellen Goodman and Patricia O'Brien

Best Friends: The Pleasures and Perils of Girls' and Women's Friendships by Terri Apter and Ruthellen Josselon

Maskmaking by Carole Sivin

Breaking Free by Marilyn Sewell

Girls Like Us by Gina Misiroglu

Chapter 4: Remembering

What does "remembering" mean to you? In Chapter 4, we learn that to remember is to recognize that our identity is connected to a larger universe than we had previously known. The suggested exercises for this chapter are meant to aid us in our remembering, thus deepening our connection to all things.

Suggestions:
- The facilitator poses the reflection questions at the end of Chapter 4 (page 54). Women share their answers.

- Talk about a time during your childhood when you realized something beyond what you had been taught. How did that moment affect you?
- The facilitator reads aloud *Three Times My Life Has Opened* by Jane Hirschfield (page 43). Women take turns discussing their reactions to it and sharing ways their own lives have opened.
- The facilitator reads aloud the passage from *A Sketch of the Past* by Virginia Woolf (page 47). Women take turns discussing their reactions to it.
- Take twenty minutes to write about the most powerful time in your life when you were in touch with something that seemed transcendent. This may have been an out-of-body experience or a time when you saw something beyond life's everyday limits. Read these memories aloud.

Recommended Reading

A Woman's Book of Life by Joan Borysenko

Awakening the Heroes Within: Twelve Archetypes to Help Us Find Ourselves and Transform Our World by Carol S. Pearson

Circle of Stones by Judith Durek

Chapter 5: Exploring

Chapter 5 invites us to explore new ways to experience ourselves, to engage in ideas that can enhance our lives. As we tap into our potential as creative beings, we discover new answers to old questions. These suggested exercises are offered in the spirit of exploring.

Suggestions:
- The facilitator poses the reflection questions at the end of Chapter 5 (page 65). Women share their answers.
- Each woman could inquire into the traditional aspects of her religion of origin, as well as the more esoteric branches of this religion, and share her findings with the group. If a member was raised nonreligiously or no longer practices in that faith, she

might explore other means of understanding spirituality (such as through nature, poetry, or art).

- Make collages using magazines and photos that represent each stage of the journey. Seena Frost's "Soul Collages" and the "Soul-cards" by Deborah Koff-Chapin each facilitate new spiritual insights, and are ideal to work with in women's circles.
- The facilitator reads aloud *Peonies at Dusk* by Jane Kenyon (page 63). Women take turns discussing their reactions to it.
- Painting a mandala has historically been used as a way to explore one's inner psyche and universal themes. Set aside an evening to work with mandalas, using colored pencils or felt tip markers. You can find books from the library on mandalas, or purchase mandala coloring books.

Recommended Reading

The Woman's Encyclopedia of Myths and Secrets by Barbara Walker

Where People Fly and Water Runs Uphill: Using Dreams to Tap the Wisdom of the Unconscious by Jeremy Taylor

Everyone's Mandala Coloring Book Vol. I by Monique Mandali

Life, Paint and Passion by Michele Cassou

The Dance of Ecstasy by Jalaja Bonheim

The Nine Muses by Angeles Arrien

Chapter 6: Practicing

Being in a women's circle is a practice of open-mindedness, intention, honesty, commitment, and accountability. With the help of witnesses, we are encouraged to walk in this human life more in touch with spirit, more connected to our essence. The suggested exercises for Chapter 6 are to help us define and explore practice.

Suggestions:
- The facilitator poses the reflection questions at the end of Chapter 6 (page 73). Women share their answers.

- The facilitator reads aloud the passages regarding the *Four-Fold Way* (pages 69). Women take turns discussing their reactions to each of the four steps. Then, taking a personal relationship in their lives that has troubling aspects, each woman explores how using the Four Fold Plan as a practice might change that relationship.
- Spend 15–25 minutes doing a guided visualization. Share feelings about the experience. Discuss any resistance to the exercise.
- This exercise helps turn anger into something useful through practice. Each woman completes the sentence below, reads it aloud and makes a commitment, and practices making a difference by committing to an action:

Something that goes on in the world that I feel really angry about is:

The worst part about it is:

Every time I read an article or hear someone talk about it, I feel:

I think that what needs to be done is:

What stops me from trying to make a difference is:

One thing I could do over the next three months would be:

If I were to make a commitment to use this as a practice I would begin by:

I will commit to _____ by the time the group meets next.

Recommended Reading

The Four-Fold Way: Walking the Paths of the Warrior, Teacher, Healer, and Visionary by Angeles Arrien

The Vein of Gold: A Journey to Your Creative Heart by Julia Cameron

The Artist's Way by Julia Cameron

The Force of Kindness by Sharon Salzberg

Chapter 7: Shadows on the Path

As we continue over time with our women's circle, we will find shadows on the path that show themselves within the women's group.

Right alongside our best, soulful self come the deep-seated elements of ego, with all ego's envious, competitive, inadequate, shy, judging, and oversensitive proclivities. These elements are essential to explore, and they will doubtlessly play a role in the group's dynamics. All of the issues that have ever come up in your life with other women will come up in the circle. The longer you are together, the more strongly you will feel them. Having a practice in place to deal with the possible trouble is very important in creating a long-lasting, successful group. The suggested exercises for Chapter 7 are to help us look at the shadows on the path.

Suggestions:

- The facilitator poses the reflection questions at the end of Chapter 7 (page 83). Women share their answers.
- Begin by reading this description of judgment by Hal and Sidra Stone: "Whomever we judge or whatever we judge is an expression of one or more of our disowned selves." How might we apply this insight to our own lives? Who or what do we judge, and what does that tell us about ourselves?
- Have every woman choose one of the following ideas presented in Chapter 7 that has meaning for her and write a paragraph of reflection. Have them read their reflections aloud.

- "The Myth of Enlightenment" (page 75).
- "The Secret Club" (page 77).
- "The Doctrine of Dualism" (page 78).
- "The Spiritual Emergency" (page 79).

Recommended Reading

God Is No Laughing Matter: Observations and Objections on the Spiritual Path by Julia Cameron

Dark Side of the Light Chasers by Debbie Ford

Meeting the Shadow by Connie Zweig

Loving What Is by Byron Katie

Chapter 8: Reclaiming

In the circle, we are empowered to reclaim our essence with the support and encouragement of others. In a world that may have little time for spiritual realization, a women's circle is a precious place of connectedness, humor, safety, and focus. As we get further in touch with our own essence, it is helpful to have witnesses that validate the more authentic ways we are learning to live our lives. Normal life passages, trials, and even positive accomplishments are all opportunities to reclaim connection to all parts of our lives. The suggested exercises for Chapter 8 are intended to empower us as we reclaim our essence.

Suggestions:

- The facilitator poses the reflection questions at the end of Chapter 8 (page 90). Women share their answers.
- Each woman names one part of her she wishes to reclaim in her life. She talks about three *concrete* ways she will work on this. "I am going to reclaim my artist," as an expression of intention, is not concrete. Instead, she can say, "I want to reclaim the artist in me. I will keep a journal and draw in it three times a week. I will take a life drawing class at the community college next fall, and I will stop telling myself I am not an artist."

- The facilitator reads aloud the poem by May Sarton (page 87). Women take turns discussing their reactions to it.
- Ask each woman to bring in photographs and stories about a woman they admire. It may be their great-grandmother Nellie, or Sojourner Truth, or a present-day figure such as Oprah Winfrey. Each woman will show photos and tell the story of the woman they selected, describing the reason this woman's story spoke to them. The final part of the exercise is for the presenter to acknowledge how she has the same "gold" as the woman she chose.
- Honor the Goddess as a metaphor for female spirituality. Taking turns, one at a time, each woman sits in a chair in the middle of the circle. Going around the circle, each woman shares heartfelt admiration and gratitude for the woman in the center.

Recommended Reading

Meetings with Remarkable Women: Buddhist Teachers in America by Lenore Friedman

Faith and Feminism: A Holy Alliance by Helen Hunt, Ph.D.

When Things Fall Apart, Heart Advice for Difficult Times by Pema Chodron

Wise Women: A Celebration of Their Insights, Courage, and Beauty by Joyce Tenneson

Chapter 9: Acceptance

Our circle encourages us to greet change with a peaceful heart of acceptance. But more than this, we need to accept that we will forget everything we have learned at times, and this must be met with compassion and acceptance. The suggested exercises for Chapter 9 help us work toward acceptance.

Suggestions:
- The facilitator poses the reflection questions at the end of Chapter 9 (page 97). Women share their answers.

- The group spends twenty minutes writing about a moment or event that changed their lives in the form of a fairy-tale or myth. Take turns reading the stories aloud.
- Write your life in a time line that indicates trouble spots. Look at the difficult times you have been through. Now think of who you are as a result of dealing with those troubles. If you had to go back to who you were before these difficult times, would you? What might you have gained from these experiences?
- Read aloud a copy of the poem "I Go Back To May" by Sharon Olds, then share what meaning it has for you regarding acceptance.
- Read aloud one of "The Rules for Being Human" developed by Cherie Carter Scott, Ph.D. (listed below). Share about when you learned this lesson.

Rule # 1

YOU WILL RECEIVE A BODY.
You may love it or hate it, but it will be yours for the duration of your life on Earth.

Rule # 2

YOU WILL BE PRESENTED WITH LESSONS.
You are enrolled in a full-time informal school called "life." Each day in this school you will have the opportunity to learn lessons. You may like the lessons or hate them, but you have designed them as part of your curriculum.

Rule # 3

THERE ARE NO MISTAKES, ONLY LESSONS.
Growth is a process of experimentation, a series of trials, errors, and occasional victories. The failed experiments are as much a part of the process as the experiments that work.

Rule # 4

A LESSON IS REPEATED UNTIL LEARNED.

Lessons will be repeated to you in various forms until you have learned them. When you have learned them, you can then go on to the next lesson.

Rule # 5

LEARNING DOES NOT END.

There is no part of life that does not contain lessons. If you are alive, there are lessons to be learned.

Rule # 6

"THERE" IS NO BETTER THAN "HERE."

When your "there" has become a "here," you will simply obtain a "there" that will look better to you than your present "here."

Rule # 7

OTHERS ARE ONLY MIRRORS OF YOU.

You cannot love or hate something about another person unless it reflects something you love or hate about yourself.

Rule # 8

WHAT YOU MAKE OF YOUR LIFE IS UP TO YOU.

You have all the tools and resources you need. What you do with them is up to you.

Rule # 9

YOUR ANSWERS LIE INSIDE YOU.

All you need to do is look, listen, and trust.

Rule # 10

YOU WILL FORGET ALL THIS AT BIRTH.

You can remember if you want by unraveling the double-helix of inner knowledge.

Recommended Reading

Grace (Eventually): Thoughts on Faith by Anne Lamott
Crones Don't Whine: Concentrated Wisdom for Juicy Women by Jean Shinoda Bolen
The Search for the Beloved by Jean Houston

A woman's journey begins and ends against the backdrop of a "babble" of women searching for freedom, self-expression, and knowledge. Whether our feet are covered in rags, shod in boots, high heels, or Birkenstocks, we work now, as we have always worked, in circles of support both seen and unseen. The patterns of women wounding, betraying, and fearing one another are broken as we recover the possibilities that existed before we were, as writer Tillie Olsen puts it, "misshapen; crucified into a sex, a color, a walk of life, a nationality."

The oldest ritual among women is sharing stories, trials, and musings: at rivers and streams and around fires; at the kitchen table, over the fence, and on the telephone; in temples, churches, and mosques. We speak of our passage from one stage of life to another, from menstruation through menopause, and all that happens in between. We seek and provide comfort and wisdom to each other. We challenge one another. We wound and help to heal one another. We hold each others' hands in times of trouble. In the shared space we create together, new parts of us are stirred awake. Witnessing the journey of others toward their deepest selves, with this book as guide, can help us reconnect with this essential energy so often missing from our daily lives. Together, we begin to explore one of the most unfathomable mysteries of all: the mystery of who we really are.

How might your life have been different, if, through the years, there had been a place where you could go? . . . A place of women, away from the ordinary busy-ness of life . . . a place of women who knew the cycles of life, the ebb and flow of nature, who knew of times of work and times of quiet . . . who understood your tiredness and need for rest. A place of women who could help you to accept your fatigue and trust

your limitations, and to know, in the dark of winter, that your energy would return, as surely as the spring. Women who could help you learn to light a candle and to wait. How might your life be different?
— JUDITH DUERK, *CIRCLE OF STONES: WOMAN'S JOURNEY*
  TO HERSELF

There is a door. It opens. Then it is closed. But a slip of light stays, like a scrap of unreadable paper left on the floor, or the one red leaf the snow releases in March.
— JANE HIRSHFIELD, FROM "THREE TIMES MY LIFE HAS OPENED"

Acknowledgments

Judy Carroll and Larry Backstedt introduced me to poetry when I was twelve years old. Neither of them are here in body, but their spirits resound in me every day. Karen Randall, my best friend of fifty years, helped me see poetry as a form of prayer. Susan Hawthorne and Burke Hunter have been unfaltering and inspiring kin and I cannot imagine my life without them.

This book would not have been possible without the constant encouragement, humor, willingness, and hundreds of hours in dialogue of Ann Ladd, my colleague and dear friend. Thanks to the poets who have so generously allowed their work to be reprinted here. Your words inspire and move me.

I have been blessed with incredible mentors: Angeles Arrien, Jacqueline Small, Sidra and Hal Stone, Father Eugene, Shallert S. J., Lori Gordon, Harville Hendrix and Helen Hunt, and Stan and Christina Grof, to name just a few. The work of A. H. Almaas has moved me profoundly.

Karen Ruckman was undeterred in her determination to find a home for this book, and I am very indebted for her ideas and editing, and her inspiring photographs, which were a part of the first manuscript of this book. Brenda Knight was a generous and most enthusiastic editor, Caroline Pincus was grounded, wise, and supportive as an editor, and I appreciate Caroline Herter for her persistence as an agent.

Thanks to Marie France, Tim Head, and Carolyn Mondress for assistance with editing and revising. Doris Ober was the magician who often turned an ordinary passage into an inspiring one. Margaret Ronda's intelligence and skill have made this a better book.

Suze Bear came into my life at the perfect moment, when I needed organization, wit, and the abilities of someone who truly "got it." She has helped bring this project to completion with unbelievable support and skill.

Tim Barraud, my husband of twenty years, my dearest friend of thirty-three years, calls me to "Remember" my best self again and again.

Credits and Permissions

About the Author

Linda Carroll was born in San Francisco in 1944 and adopted into an Italian Catholic family. Very early, she discovered poetry as a form of prayer and a window into an expanded life. In 1961, when Linda graduated from high school, San Francisco was already buzzing with counterculture music, arts, and style, and Linda found herself selling beads and going to peace marches. After finishing her bachelor's degree in Oregon in the 1970s, Linda moved to New Zealand, where she raised children, sheep, and many dogs. She then returned to Oregon, received a masters in counseling, and began practicing as a therapist. About 15 years ago, she and her veterinarian husband, Tim Barraud, began to teach a couples course based on the Imago work of Harville Hendrix, the Pairs training of Dr. Lori Gordon, and their own insights, study, and practices. They continue to offer retreats and seminars all over the world, and Linda is currently at work on a book project, *Love's Four Journeys*, based on this work.

As an adult, Linda found her birth mother, the novelist Paula Fox, and began to understand her deep-seated love of poetry anew. In 2006, her memoir, *Her Mother's Daughter*, was published by Doubleday. She has five children, ten grandchildren, and lives in Corvallis, Oregon, with her husband, two Jack Russell terriers and a Siamese cat, and continues her lifelong path of spiritual seeking.

When Linda began writing this book, she realized that the poems which had been her steady companions throughout her life beautifully illuminated the various stages of a woman's life journey.

You can visit Linda at *lindacarroll.org*.

To Our Readers

Conari Press, an imprint of Red Wheel/Weiser, publishes books on topics ranging from spirituality, personal growth, and relationships to women's issues, parenting, and social issues. Our mission is to publish quality books that will make a difference in people's lives—how we feel about ourselves and how we relate to one another. We value integrity, compassion, and receptivity, both in the books we publish and in the way we do business.

Our readers are our most important resource, and we value your input, suggestions, and ideas about what you would like to see published. Please feel free to contact us, to request our latest book catalog, or to be added to our mailing list.

Conari Press
An imprint of Red Wheel/Weiser, LLC
500 Third Street, Suite 230
San Francisco, CA 94107
www.redwheelweiser.com